"What the world sees as adversity, God sees as an opportunity for blessing. Stephanie Hubach has discovered this, as I have with my fifteen-year-old autistic grandson, Max. In this book Stephanie makes a very important contribution to equipping the church for its ministry to people with disabilities and their families. It is well rooted theologically and, to my delight, grows out of her well-formed biblical worldview. I hope it will be used as a tool by churches to minister to the least of these—and in the process to reflect God's glorious Kingdom."

—CHARLES W. COLSON, Founder and Chairman, Prison Fellowship

"Stephanie Hubach masterfully and winsomely develops a scriptural framework to help God's people think biblically and live convenantally in all of life, including our response to disabilities."

—SUSAN HUNT, Author and Consultant, Christian Education and Publications, Presbyterian Church in America

"Her superb book tells us how to transform the church into a place of hospitality and welcome for children and adults with disabilities and their families. The starting point of this transformation is the gift of genuine friendship. Heartwarming stories and discussion of a biblical view of disability make this book both pleasurable and instructive."

—GINNY THORNBURGH, Director, Religion and Disability Program, National Organization on Disability

" 'Do *you* love Jesus?' asked the young man with Down syndrome, peering intently into the face of each elder in the room. If *you* love Jesus, Stephanie Hubach's book *Same Lake, Different Boat* is the book for you. While writing about coming alongside individuals and families touched by disability, she has actually penned a call for the church to become an inclusive community for all people, a 'hospital for sinners,' where justice, mercy, and grace set people free to become God's true body. If your family, like ours, is touched by having a 'least of these my brethren' member, you will resonate with Stephanie's understanding of the peculiar challenges, dynamics, and opportunities that come with having disability as an uninvited guest. If disability has not yet become your experience, this book will catapult your growth as a son or daughter of the Most High, and will galvanize you to see and to foster true community."

— JOSEPH "SKIP" AND BARBARA RYAN, Senior Pastor and wife, Park Cities Presbyterian Church, Dallas

"I have not been this excited about a book in 38 years of disability ministry! Steph Hubach draws on her tremendous love for the Lord and for people with disabilities to present a compelling challenge to include people with disabilities in the life of the church. I cannot recommend this book more highly."

—TIMOTHY D. SHEETZ, Director, Handi*Vangelism Ministries International

"*Same Lake, Different Boat* is a heart-wrenching book by an author who has lived its message. It will equip you . . . to serve as instruments of healing and hope, to accept the reality of disability with joy and thanksgiving, and to appreciate the privilege of loving people with disabilities. Stephanie Hubach has given us a goldmine from a solidly biblical and theological perspective. This book is about ministry, caring, listening, coming alongside, and helping. This book is priority reading for every leader in the church, as well as families of the disabled."

—CHARLES H. DUNAHOO, Coordinator, Christian Education and Publications, Presbyterian Church in America

"Steph has given a great gift to the church. She calls on the faithful congregation to look at and identify with persons with disabilities who are part of the church. She uses Scripture and personal family vignettes to reinforce the value of all persons. Her discussion teasing out the distinctions between a normal and abnormal world and the normal and abnormal results we live with is worth the price of the book."

—GEORGE B. STOLTZFUS, M.D., CEO, Friendship Community

"Stephanie Hubach's thoughtful challenge to the Christian community is strong but full of grace, clearly articulating our biblical responsibility to nurture individuals and families with special needs. She balances our need to rely on one another for help with our mandate to look for and celebrate every individual's dignity and giftedness. She assures us that God is not afraid of hard questions."

—PAMELA A. HARMON, Associate Director, Young Life's Capernaum Ministries

"Stephanie Hubach clearly explains in her well-written, and insightful book how we can extend our hands and hearts to people with disabilities. Stephanie wonderfully reminds us that grace enters into our lives in the most unexpected ways. I highly recommend this spiritually sound and practical book."

—CHRISTOPHER DE VINCK, Author, *The Power of the Powerless*

"Stephanie Hubach has given the church a good gift to equip the church in ministry to and with people with disabilities. It is set apart by its vision, strong theological and biblical worldview, and the gift of laughter. The reader is given a window into a family who, though touched by disability, is living, loving, and growing, in their love for Christ, one another, and his church . . . a must-read."

—JANE PATETE, Women's Ministries Coordinator, Presbyterian Church in America

"*Same Lake, Different Boat* is an exciting read. Veteran disability ministers will be refreshed by new insights, beginning workers will be inspired by the concepts, and church leaders will receive clear purpose for disability ministry."
—JIM PIERSON, Author, Speaker, and President of The Christian Church Foundation for the Handicapped

"What should the Church look like? How should the gospel shape our lives, our relationships, our worship, and our communities? In this wonderful book, Steph Hubach offers us a glimpse of what should be, what could be, what would be, if only the riches of God's grace would fully captivate us. Biblical and practical, *Same Lake, Different Boat* beautifully demonstrates the great paradox: in the Kingdom the least and the last are in fact the first and the foremost."
—GEORGE GRANT, Author and Co-Pastor for Ministries of Christ Community Church, PCA

"Stephanie Hubach's stories of her son will delight you. How she weaves those into a solid biblical framework will encourage you. Everyone who *doesn't have* a disabled child should read this book!"
—PAUL MILLER, Author, *Love Walked Among Us: Learning to Love Like Jesus*; Director, seeJesus.net.

same lake,
different boat

same lake,
different boat

Coming Alongside People
Touched by Disability

Stephanie O. Hubach

Foreword by Joni Eareckson Tada

PUBLISHING
P.O. BOX 817 • PHILLIPSBURG • NEW JERSEY 08865-0817

Library of Congress Cataloging-in-Publication Data

Hubach, Stephanie O., 1960–
    Same lake, different boat : coming alongside people touched by disability / Stephanie O. Hubach ; foreword by Joni Eareckson Tada.
        p. cm.
    Includes bibliographical references
    ISBN-10: 1-59638-051-9 (paper)
    ISBN-13: 978-1-59638-051-6 (paper)
        1. Church work with people with disabilities. 2. Disabilities—Religious aspects—Christianity. I. Title.
BV4460.H83 2006
261.8'324—dc22

                                    2006043288

In honor of my parents,
Darrah and Everett Opdahl,
who have so faithfully modeled for me
the love of God, love for neighbor, and a loving family

Contents

Foreword   9
Acknowledgments   13
Introduction   15

Part 1: About the Foundations
  1. On Truth: *The Four Missing Words*   21
  2. On Identification: *Same Lake, Different Boat*   33
  3. On Respect: *Common Grace, Special Needs*   43
  4. On Relentlessness: *Dante's Circles of Disability*   53
  5. On Restoration: *Thy Kingdom Come*   67

Part 2: About the Families
  6. On Coming to Terms with a New Reality   81
  7. On Negotiating a Path to Acceptance   97
  8. On Living a New Normal Life   113
  9. On Grappling with the Great Opportunity   133

Part 3: About Facilitation in the Church
  10. On Hospitality: *No Room at the Inn*   151
  11. On Belonging: *Same Body, Different Parts*   169
  12. On Wisdom: *Questions Every Church Needs to Answer*   187
  13. On Change: *Revolution or Reformation?*   209

Notes   227
Glossary   231

Foreword

People often ask me, "Who are your role models? Who inspires you?" I know they expect me to say Billy Graham or Amy Carmichael, but my role models are a little less lofty. Like my friend David. He uses a wheelchair and gets up extra early to take the public paratransit to church on Sunday mornings. Or Margaret, a single mom in a wheelchair who raises two young children, plus finds time to lead a women's neighborhood prayer group. Then there's Jeff and Jane, who are bending over backward to provide a sense of normalcy to their three children, all of whom are slowly dying of a degenerative muscular disease.

These people are saints who breathe celestial air. They show me what it means to follow in Christ's steps, endure hardship like a good soldier, welcome trials as friends, and rejoice in suffering. I sometimes forget how to do that. When that happens, I have David, Margaret, Jeff, and Jane to reignite my passion.

Even when they wrestle through discouragement, I am helped! I simply cannot stand—or sit—idly by. Their courage and perseverance inexorably drag me into the middle of their circumstances, challenging me to come alongside and practice Christianity with its sleeves rolled up. I'm *helped* by that. I'm all the richer, all the better for it.

It's a Polaroid snapshot of the way the church should be. When the bus doesn't let off David on Sunday mornings, our whole church knows it. And we, as a body, move into action. David enriches the congregation—perhaps more than he or the people in the pews realize. His participation in our midst is not just expanding "disability ministry"; it's changing the character of our church. He provides the inescapable reason our people serve, and do so sacrificially. Our whole church is stronger for it.

I wish more of my brothers and sisters in Christ could experience this heartwarming and potent exchange between families affected by disability and those who are, well . . . affected by other things. I'm convinced such relationships alter the landscape of the American church. But how do you make those relationships happen? I can't force people to get engaged with David, Jeff or Jane, or Margaret and her children; only the Holy Spirit can do that.

This is why *Same Lake, Different Boat* is so timely. I have read more "how to" books on disability ministry than I care to mention, but Stephanie Hubach's work is *different*. It goes deep. It speaks to our *relationships*—with God, with each other, and especially with those we're not typically drawn to (that's the important part). The book you hold in your hands will not only enlighten your thinking, but will speak to your heart and spirit, as well as open your eyes to the Jeffs and Janes in your world. You, too, will be pulled inescapably by the Spirit to embrace those the Savior especially loved when he walked on earth.

I have sat under Stephanie's teaching at our Joni and Friends workshops. As a mother of a child with Down syndrome, she speaks with authority. She's *been* there. It's why I listened so intently. As Stephanie spoke, I so wished my quadriplegic hands were able to scribble down all the fresh insights (I'd share a few here, but I don't want to spill the beans).

Stephanie has a high goal. She seeks the best for the bride of Christ. She asks us to move into relationships with people with disabilities. She underscores how we can find much greater joy in treating everyone as citizens of equal standing in Christ's kingdom. *Same Lake, Different Boat* is about the hope that she and I share: that Christ's church will someday embrace all of its members. As Chuck Swindoll told his congregation one day, "Disabled people are not in our way; they are a part of our way."

Actually, I would rephrase that. They *are* the way to creating a caring church that truly reflects the love of Christ, as well as his power. It will happen when we consider weaker members as indispensable. After all, God's power shows up best in weakness. It's something I think about every time I see David get off the bus and wheel into church.

Joni Eareckson Tada
Founder, Joni and Friends
Spring 2006

Acknowledgments

My first expression of gratitude goes to my local church family at Reformed Presbyterian Church of Ephrata. Without their willingness to heed the Scripture's call to ministries of mercy and justice—preached so faithfully by our pastors, Rev. Thomas E. Nicholas and Dr. William L. Graybill II—there would not have been a book for me to write. I am sincerely thankful for the elders, deacons, Special Needs Committee members, and The Explorers Sunday school class. Their collective desire to be a family of grace-based learners who seek to be faithful to the gospel, in word and deed, is truly inspiring.

In the larger Lancaster County Christian community I am indebted to my fellow partners in disability ministry who have been my teachers, and yet have been willing to allow me to serve alongside them as a leader in this arena. To my friends at Friendship Community, Handi*Vangelism Ministries International, Joni and Friends of Eastern PA, Love INC of Lancaster, and No Longer Alone Ministries—I extend my genuine thanks.

As a member of the Presbyterian Church in America (PCA), I would like to express my heartfelt gratitude to Jane Patete, Susan Hunt, Barbara Thompson, Charles Dunahoo, and Joni Eareckson Tada for their invaluable assistance in helping me to secure a publisher, and for regularly validating to me the importance of this project. I deeply appreciate them. I would also like to thank Fred Marsh for his unwavering support of, and vision for, disability ministry in the denomination.

Without my devoted editor, Thomas A. Nicholas, I would still be buried alive in a myriad of technical details. For his excellent skills, his great wisdom and insight, his good humor, and the immense gift of his time—I am inestimably thankful. I will miss having a regular excuse to visit with Tom and his lovely wife, Emily, who always showered me with gracious hospitality during our editing sessions. I plan to continue to visit regularly, if only to listen to Tom's latest corny jokes while I watch Emily roll her eyes in feigned disbelief. Through the process of writing this book, they have truly become my friends, and I love and respect them both.

For all of my readers, who are too numerous to list, "you know who you are." Their honest comments have made this a much better book than it would have been otherwise. In addition, their encouraging feedback motivated me to keep writing even when I was uncertain that the manuscript would ever see the light of day beyond the hard drive of my computer.

Finally, I want to thank my family. My parents, Darrah and Everett Opdahl, and my parents-in-law, Fred and Wilma Hubach, have been four of my greatest cheerleaders. My precious sons Freddy and Timmy—who have matured into Fred and Tim while I've been writing this book—well, I love them more than they will ever know. They have been tremendously good sports: willing for me to share their stories, helping around the house, and simply being the fascinating and wonderful young men they each are. They make their mother proud! Last but certainly not least, I owe my deepest appreciation to my beloved husband Fred, who—countless times—assured me, "*Yes*, I think you should keep writing. And *yes*, I'm sure it will be published." In response to my anxious queries of "How do you *know*?" he always smiled and patiently replied, "I just know." Our hearts beat as one for our God, our children, and the ministries we engage in together. Truly, what more could I ask for?

Introduction

Those who are closest to me know that one of my greatest desires in life is to understand and to be understood. While, in my best moments, that can be a wonderful gift, in my worst moments that same passion can be excessive. I like to understand life, I like to understand others, I like to understand myself—and when all is said and done, I love being able to explain what I have come to realize. Agreeing to write a book, therefore, has caused me at times to tremble in fear. While permanently printing one's thoughts onto paper surely affords the potential opportunity to be understood by a large audience, at the same time it poses tremendous risks of being seriously misinterpreted. However, I have decided—that when it comes to identifying with and ministering alongside people touched by disability—it is worth the risk.

Why write another book on disability? Aren't there enough books out there already? Yes and no. For the most part, the available Christian literature on disability could be divided into several categories. The first group consists of the experiential books. These are the stories that attempt to help the reader identify with the challenges that the writer has experienced. The second set includes motivational texts. These are the books that attempt to convince the reader of all the reasons *why* disability ministry is important in the life of the church. Finally, there are publications that are programmatic in nature. These are the practical manuals on *how* to establish programmatic ministries on behalf of individuals who are disabled.

Each of these types of books has made a wonderful contribution to the collection of available resources. What I hope to offer, however, is an innovative alternative. And a different outcome requires a different approach. As a result, this book is not an inspirational book per se, or an A-B-C how-to volume. Neither is it a bird's-eye view into the unprocessed, raw emotions of my family's experience with disability—even though much of the manuscript was written through tears. Instead, it is the compilation of what we have come to understand is *true* as a result of actively engaging in the struggle. Our intentional wrestling with God and his Word, with the realities of family life, and with the all-too-frequent inadequacies of the broader Christian community's response has brought us to a place of resolution and understanding that is positively portrayed in the text as a vision for a better way:

- A better way to understand disability biblically.
- A better way to understand the challenges that face individuals and families touched by disability.
- A better way to understand the role of the church in the lives of people with differing abilities.

That does not in any way diminish the reality of the struggle that my family has engaged in to arrive at such a place. It simply means that the focus of this book is on a vision for the future, not the pain of the past.

One of the unique gifts that God has given my family is the ability to laugh at ourselves. God has used the entrance of disability into my world as a refining fire that has profoundly changed how I view and value others and myself. It has caused me to be deeply convicted of my need for grace, and at the same time it has encouraged me to embrace God's grace and "lighten up." Throughout the book you will meet my family. They are the delight of my life. My older son, Freddy (now age 16), is academically gifted, relatively serious, philosophically reflective, and immensely caring. Timmy (now age 14)—my younger son who has Down syndrome—is bright in his own unique way, has a hilarious sense of humor, is occasionally very impulsive, and is quite the encourager. Fred, my patient and loving husband, is a deeply warm and practical man in both faith and practice. He is truly my best friend, gently bringing balance to my passion, intensity, and vision in our shared life. The relational dynamics of our family that occur around our dinner table, at the grocery store, and in the church parking lot are enough to—at times—send me into simultaneous gales of laughter and rivers of tears. In the context of this book, the stories I tell about my children are simply used as bridges to the world of truth that I hope you will come to understand. Such tales are not intended to be universally representative of *every* individual's or family's experience of living with disability—not even representative of most—for that is quite literally impossible. Disability covers a huge spectrum, and both individual temperaments and family personalities are diverse. But the specific realities to which the stories about Freddy and Timmy point are, I believe, universal truths. It is my hope that you will embrace these truths, either better than before or, perhaps, for the first time.

This book is intended as a gift to the church. May it be received in the same generous spirit with which it is offered. And most of all, by God's grace, may it make a positive difference.

To God be the glory,
Stephanie O. Hubach
Spring 2006

PART 1

About the Foundations

1

On Truth: The Four Missing Words

Truth and the morning become light with time.
—South African Proverb

It was truly the quintessential spring day, balmy and seventy-two degrees, in Timonium, Maryland, on April 30, 1983. A gentle rain shower had passed through in the morning and now warm sunshine bathed the sanctuary of Timonium Presbyterian Church. Resonating from the voice of the tenor soloist came this beautiful prayer:

> O Lord Most Holy,
> O Lord Most Holy,
> O Loving Father, Thee would we be praising always.
> Help us to know Thee,
> Know Thee and love Thee;
> Father, Father, grant us Thy truth and grace;
> Father, Father, guide and defend us.
>
> Rule Thou our wilful hearts,
> Keep Thee our wand'ring thoughts;
> In all our sorrows let us find our rest in Thee;
> And in temptation's hour,
> Save through Thy mighty pow'r,

Thine aid O send us;
Hear us in mercy.

Show us Thy favor,
So shall we live, and sing praise to Thee.[1]

Then we pledged our vows—"I, Stephanie Darrah, take thee, Frederick Robert, . . . in joy and in sorrow . . . in plenty and in want . . . in sickness and in health"—never imagining how deeply those vows would be tested, nor how fully our wedding prayer would be answered.

Surprised by Disability

Timothy Robert Hubach was born on January 5, 1992. In retrospect, I still can't believe that I didn't anticipate the possibility. Unlike the birth of our first son just two years earlier, this delivery was rapid and intense. As I gazed at Timmy immediately after his speedy arrival, I was stunned by his appearance. Everything about him seemed different from our elder son, Freddy—*really* different. His stocky, round, and doughboy-like figure was a marked departure from the defined features of his older brother. *But then again, we have had some rather rotund relatives on both sides of the family*, I reasoned to myself. When I first held him and noticed his slanted little eyes, my own eyes darted around the delivery room to see if anyone else saw what I saw. But noticing the hospital staff going about their post-delivery tasks as usual, I dismissed my concerns as irrational. Quite uncharacteristically, I never even voiced my thoughts to my husband Fred.

I suppose my next clue might have been the remark made by a nurse early that afternoon. Timmy was sleeping soundly in the bassinet next to my bed. Having experienced an all-night labor and knowing that I was going home the next day to our extremely energetic firstborn, I was resting for the few precious hours I had left. The nurse entered my room and in a patronizing voice stated, "It's OK to *hold them*, you know." I felt irritated and annoyed by her mysterious comment, but chose to dismiss it. Soon thereafter, a doctor from our family practice group arrived on the scene. Without indicating anything specific, he came in and spoke to me in a very serious tone. His words assured me that there was probably nothing to be concerned about, but his face told the truth. He had requested the town pediatrician to come in and evaluate Timmy.

At this point it seemed as if everyone was talking *at me*, but no one was actually communicating *with me*. A theme of inexplicable sadness and solemnity hovered over the proceedings of the afternoon. Alone at the hospital while Fred was at home caring for Freddy, I felt slightly confused, and a tad lonely—all of which I attributed to the fact that I was quite fatigued.

That evening, all the events of the day finally came into focus even as the room around me began to swirl out of focus. The pediatrician entered my room and, after brief introductions, announced, "We believe that Timothy has a chromosomal abnormality." I remember feeling dizzy and disoriented, as if the physician's words were somehow being spoken through a funnel in another place. As he began to talk to me about Down syndrome,* the hot tears streamed down my face. *How could this be? I am only thirty-one years old.* Somehow I stumbled through a series of questions and answers with him. Then he turned and left. Sobbing alone in the darkness, I entertained the bizarre thought, *I wonder if I should tell Fred. Maybe I'll call him tomorrow.* Mind, body, and soul—I was already in a state of shock. Eight simple words had been spoken by the pediatrician, yet I knew instinctively that our lives would never be the same.

* "Down syndrome is a genetic condition that causes delays in physical and intellectual development. It occurs in approximately one in every 800 live births. Individuals with Down syndrome have 47 chromosomes instead of the usual 46. It is the most frequently occurring chromosomal disorder." (Source: National Down Syndrome Association)

Why didn't my husband and I anticipate the possibility? Very close friends of ours had recently become the parents of not one, but *two* sons with significant disabilities. What made us assume that we were exempt from a similar occurrence? We aren't the only ones who have been surprised by disability. In fact, surprise appears to be a nearly universal response to disability. Why is that?

Many years ago, there was a television show called *To Tell the Truth*. On the show three contestants were presented to a panel of questioners. Each of the contestants claimed to be telling the truth about his or her identity. The job of the panel was to discern who indeed was being honest. There is a game of To Tell the Truth going on with regard to disability today. In this case, there are three different views as to what is true about the nature of disability and about the nature of our world at large. Let's explore these three views and determine which is consistent with reality.

The Historical View:
Disability Is an *Abnormal* Part of Life in a *Normal* World

Throughout the ages, people with disabilities have typically been, and continue to be, seen as aberrations. They are viewed as an *abnormal* part of life in a *normal* world. This is why we are often surprised by disability: it is viewed as outside the mainstream of the expected. You've heard the questions; if we're honest, we can admit that we've all asked these questions (or at least ones similar to these):

"Pssssst! Mommy—what's *wrong* with her?"

"What's his *problem*?"

"What is that child's birth *defect*?"

What is the underlying assumption in these questions? It is this: the routine of the world in which we live is the baseline—and, therefore, that which is "normal." Differences from the norm are then regarded as something *other*—something *ab*normal. This does not have a positive connotation. It does not take much imagination to understand why people with disabilities resent being seen this way. No one wants to be defined exclusively by his or her limitations. No one wants to be considered unacceptable to the rest of the human community. Worse than that, the "abnormal part of a normal world" perspective has been the basis and even the justification for countless abuses against people with disabilities. Consider the words of a well-known disability advocate:

> Throughout history, people with physical and mental disabilities have been abandoned at birth, banished from society, used as court jesters, drowned and burned during The Inquisition, gassed in Nazi Germany, and still continue to be segregated, institutionalized, tortured in the name of behaviour management, abused, raped, euthanized, and murdered.[2]

Tragically, this is an accurate accounting. Clearly, how people are viewed affects how they are treated. The historical perspective of disability has focused almost exclusively on the distinctive, negative characteristics of the diagnosis, and very little on the reality of the shared, valuable personhood of the individual. A reaction to this imbalance has given rise to the next view: the postmodern view of disability.

The Postmodern View:
Disability Is a *Normal* Part of Life in a *Normal* World

For some time now, disability advocates have been thoroughly annoyed by the "abnormal" label slapped on those with disabling conditions. As we've just seen, there is good reason for this sense of frustration. Determined to improve the lives of people affected by disability, activists are attempting to reframe the debate. In predictable postmodern* fashion, this is being accomplished by resorting to changing the language of disability. This alteration cannot be overemphasized. If you listen carefully, you can hear the dramatically shifting terminology. Ponder these statements from the writings of a nationally known speaker at a recent Down syndrome conference:

> Having a disability is a difference like any other human characteristic. It is not a deficiency. It is by no means a tragedy and does not deserve pity or benevolence or charity. Now is the time to recognize and celebrate disability rather than ignore, devalue or use it as a justification for lower expectations.[3]

Can you feel the huge shift here? The new language confuses everything and solves nothing. Does this person really mean what she said? Is disability to be regarded with no greater acknowledgment than hair color? Of course no one wants to be an object of pity, but are people affected by disability begging to be released from the compassion of those around them? If disability is something to be celebrated, then why don't more people attempt to acquire traumatic brain injuries? In response to an appropriate desire to celebrate the *individual*, the postmodern view instead ends up celebrating the *diagnosis*.

Imagine the ramifications of this postmodern view. Suppose you had walked into my hospital room just after the town pediatrician had left. What would have occurred if you had entered, stood by my bed, and greeted me with, "Hey!

---

* *Postmodernism* is a philosophy that rejects the existence of absolute truth and the associated ability to reason on the basis of what is known to be true. Language, therefore, is not considered to be a vehicle to convey truth but, instead, is viewed as a tool that is employed so that one individual or group might exert power over another individual or group.

Isn't this great? So glad to hear of your son's diagnosis. It couldn't have happened to a nicer family! I just wish it was me!" How long do you think you would have been allowed to stay before the nurse called for the hospital security guard? Would you have walked away bewildered, thinking, *What did I say that upset her?* Or would you inherently have known that the things you said were cruel? This example may seem absurd, but that is because the "normal part of a normal world" perspective is absurd. Those who promote this new philosophy fail to, or refuse to, recognize that the deeper issue lies in our worldview—our view of the world itself. Such a perspective directly impacts how we see ourselves and others. The postmodern approach does nothing to remedy that.

The Biblical View:
Disability Is a *Normal* Part of Life in an *Abnormal* World

Those with a postmodern perspective are capturing partial truths in an inaccurate context. Disability is indeed a normal part of life as we know it. It is unpredictable but occurs with a degree of regularity. You will find people with an endless variety of disabilities in cultures of every kind across the world. This has occurred across the centuries. But does that make disability itself something celebratory? The key to understanding this is the context, and the context is the following four missing words: *in an abnormal world.* When we recognize that disability is a *normal* part of life in an *abnormal* world, we can begin to make sense of it—and ourselves. In his book *The God Who Is There* Francis Schaeffer put it this way: "It is not that philosophy and Christianity deal with completely different questions, but . . . differ in their answers—including the important point as to whether man and history are now normal or abnormal."[4]

When we begin with the biblical account of creation, we realize that everything God created was good, and mankind was deemed *very* good:

So God created man in his own image,
in the image of God he created him;
male and female he created them.

God blessed them and said to them, "Be fruitful and
increase in number; fill the earth and subdue it. Rule over
the fish of the sea and the birds of the air and over every living creature that moves on the ground." (Gen. 1:27–28)

Human beings were God's crowning act of creation. While
fashioned as creatures, people were designed to intrinsically
embody his likeness. This means that mankind has a myriad
of finite potentialities that reflect God's infinite reality.
These include the ability to love, to create, to rule, to relate,
to design, to reason, and so much more. People were
designed to reflect the essence of God's character expressed
through God-imaging capacities. According to the Genesis
account, we were fashioned to experience purposeful,
blessed lives.

But then tragedy struck. In Adam and Eve's desire to
rule, not only over the rest of creation but over themselves,
the fall of mankind occurred—adversely impacting every
aspect of creation. As Paul states in Romans 8:20, "The creation was subjected to frustration, not by its own choice."
Our world became an abnormal world. For the first time in
human experience, brokenness and difficulty were introduced. This marring of creation permeated not only the spiritual, but also the physical, the intellectual, the emotional,
the psychological, and the social. The effects continue to
carry over today into our work, our world, our bodies, and
our relationships with self, others, and God. Reflecting on
this, the apostle Paul again notes in Romans 8, "The whole
creation has been groaning" (v. 22).

What does this mean in practical terms? Does this
mean that everything in human experience is *ruined* by the
fall? Absolutely not. But it does mean that everything in

human experience is *affected* by the fall. On every level of every dimension of the human experience there is a mixture of both the blessedness of creation and the brokenness of the fall. By God's common grace, we participate in the damaged but not obliterated blessings of being created in God's image and being endowed with purpose. At the same time our experience is permeated throughout with the effects of brokenness. This is true for every person. Yet much of our energies in life are directed toward denying this reality.

For some people, the effects of brokenness are more noticeable or more dramatically experienced in one part of life over another. For example, for a person battling cancer, the impact of brokenness on the physical dimension of being human stands out in bold relief. However, all of us face the slow, incremental process of inching toward death on a daily basis. It has been said that "Health is just the slowest form of dying"—and so it is! At the same time, the person fighting cancer may be experiencing more spiritual wholeness than their counterpart who is relatively physically fit but perhaps increasingly corrupted from pursuing a blatantly immoral and self-centered lifestyle.

What does this imply, then, about disability? Disability is essentially a more noticeable form of the brokenness that is common to the human experience—a normal part of life in an abnormal world. It is just a difference of degree along a spectrum that contains difficulty all along its length. Due to God's common grace, no one exists in the extreme of complete brokenness. Due to the fall, no one enjoys the extreme of complete blessing. We all experience some mixture of the two in every aspect of our humanity—including the spiritual, the physical, the intellectual, the emotional, the psychological, and the social.

Many people with disabilities can testify that a disability in one aspect of their being has produced tremendous blessing in another aspect. Jon is an adult in our local congregation who was born with spina bifida.* Due to the nature of his condition, he uses a wheelchair and requires assistance for many daily living activities. In response to these challenges, Jon has nurtured a positive attitude, a warm sense of humor, a deep faith in Christ, and a notable quality of patience that outshines his "able-bodied" peers in many ways. As Jon testified at a Sanctity of Human Life service, "I just focus on living one day at a time, taking each day for what it brings. And God will just lead me through. Whatever I face, I'll face with Him." For Jon, physical disability† has been a catalyst for tremendous spiritual growth. He has taken something that is a *normal* part of life in an *abnormal* world, and redeemed it for God's glory.

In a comparable way, a person with Down syndrome may tend to learn more slowly or require things to be explained more concretely. However, that same attribute, which is defined by society as an intellectual disability,‡ can have beautiful spiritual ramifications that put to shame those who may be more intellectually capable. Several years ago, our family received a letter from a relief organization that contained a graphic depiction of individuals living in dire poverty. The photograph conveyed the reality of the extreme deprivation in which families attempt to scratch out an existence surrounded by shacks and boiling pots of palm oil in a barren, mud-packed place. I was so moved by the photo that I felt compelled to share it with my children that evening while we

* "Spina bifida is a neural tube defect that happens in the first month of pregnancy when the spinal column doesn't close completely." (Source: Spina Bifida Association)

† *Physical disabilities* is a broad category of disability encompassing disabilities that affect movement.

‡ *Intellectual disabilities* is the current terminology for the condition formerly referred to as mental retardation. "Mental retardation is a disability characterized by significant limitations both in intellectual functioning and in adaptive behavior as expressed in conceptual, social, and practical adaptive skills. This disability originates before the age of 18. In regard to the intellectual criterion for the diagnosis of mental retardation, mental retardation is generally thought to be present if an individual has an IQ test score of approximately 70 or below." (Source: American Association of Mental Retardation)

were sitting around the dinner table. As I displayed the picture to our two sons, both of them were visibly moved. While I was describing the root causes of this type of poverty, Timmy was silent for a moment, and then his eyebrows furrowed. Quietly and deliberately he questioned, "Do we have money? Couldn't we send them some?" Timmy's need to see things concretely is a gift in the realm of the spiritual. Guess whose family mailed a donation that week?

Truth Sets the Stage for Success

We slipped into the back row of Reformed Presbyterian Church of Ephrata during the morning announcements, with newborn Timmy tucked into the infant seat resting beside us. In contrast to our wedding day, it was a different church, in a different decade, and under very different circumstances. As we sat down we heard the words of our close friend and youth pastor, "Timothy Robert Hubach was born last Sunday morning. Fred and Steph have asked me to let you know that he was born with Down syndrome." At this point the audible gasps of our church family could be heard around the sanctuary, giving voice to the raw pain in our own hearts. "But Fred and Steph also want you to know that your condolences are not expected. Instead, they want you to celebrate with them the life of this child of the covenant." Greeted after the service by the congratulatory hugs of our teary-eyed friends, we could not imagine a more wonderful way to introduce Timmy to his church family. Even as our hearts were racked with sorrow at the diagnosis and all of its implications to Timmy's life and ours, we chose to focus on the precious value of his personhood. "Joy and sorrow . . . plenty and want . . . sickness and health." This is the stuff of disability, which is simply the stuff of life. It's time To Tell the Truth about disability: it is a normal part of life in an abnormal world. We are all recipients of the blessedness of creation and the brokenness of the fall. Upholding a biblical perspective of disability really

31

matters, because when we see our world truthfully, we can view ourselves more correctly. When we view ourselves more correctly, we can also regard others more accurately. And when we regard others more accurately, we are more likely to respond to them appropriately.

As the South African proverb states: "Truth and the morning become light with time." Well, it's time.

Personal Application Questions

1. If you are honest with yourself, which worldview perspective of disability dominates your thinking? Is it the historical view, the postmodern view, or the biblical view?

2. Why does a biblical view of disability allow us to grieve the diagnosis of a person's disabling condition while celebrating the individual at the same time?

3. In what ways have you personally experienced the blessings of creation and the brokenness of the fall in different areas of your life?

4. How does accurately perceiving disability as a "normal part of life in an abnormal world" hold the potential to improve the lives of those touched by disability?

2

On Identification:
Same Lake, Different Boat

Identify: to associate or affiliate oneself closely with a person or group —The American Heritage Dictionary

Bearing down on the pedals intently, I strained to maneuver my bike up one of the steepest hills in town, weaving back to the safety of our house. The weather was hot, hot, hot—one of those incredibly scorching summer days when the heat radiates off the pavement in waves, making the task of cycling all the more arduous. Anyone watching from the outside would have observed that I was simply attempting to ride a bicycle. But truth be known, on the inside I was running. Running away. Having just moved to a small, rural Pennsylvania town from the fast-paced environment of a defense consulting job in Washington, D.C., I had been trying to find a constructive way to fill my time until I found new employment. After working sixty-hour weeks while completing my master's degree, I was attempting to slow down a bit and lead a more balanced life that included more time with my husband and other people, and less time with data and spreadsheets.

On this particular day, I had decided to visit a local personal care home. In Pennsylvania, personal care homes provide housing for individuals who do not need intensive nursing care, but cannot live unassisted for any number of reasons. This means that they often house people with a variety of special needs, including those with cognitive disabilities,* mental illness,† or physical disabilities. However, I didn't know any of that. I just thought there would be a few neatly dressed and mentally alert elderly people who were sitting around watching TV, but were secretly waiting for the chance to engage in a stimulating conversation or a rousing game of checkers with me.

Needless to say, I was shocked at what I saw . . . and what I smelled . . . and what I heard. Upon opening the front door, I was greeted by a long, dark, dingy hallway, and the smell of soiled diapers, and the sounds of human woe. Although sensing that perhaps I had underestimated what I was getting myself into, I still cheerfully marched into the administrator's office and offered to visit with anyone who was available. After looking at me somewhat curiously, the woman directed me down the hallway to a room with a vaulted ceiling where I was seated with a man named Paul, whose wife had recently died. The staff thought perhaps my visit could help cheer him up. I had no idea what to say to him. He dutifully answered my questions as we sat in the center of this room surrounded by people with various disabilities slumped in their recliners, in wheelchairs, and on couches. I couldn't wait to leave. After fifteen minutes elapsed, I had

---

* "'Cognitive disabilities' is often used by physicians, neurologists, psychologists and other professionals to include adults sustaining head injuries with brain trauma after age 18, adults with infectious diseases or affected by toxic substances leading to organic brain syndromes and cognitive deficits after age 18, and with older adults with Alzheimer diseases or other forms of dementias as well as other populations that do not meet the strict definition of mental retardation." Thus, *cognitive disabilities* is an "umbrella" term that includes intellectual disabilities (formerly referred to as mental retardation) but is broader than intellectual disabilities alone. (Source: U.S. Administration on Developmental Disabilities)

† "A mental illness is a disease that causes mild to severe disturbances in thought and/or behavior, resulting in an inability to cope with life's ordinary demands and routines. There are more than two hundred classified forms of mental illness. Some of the more common disorders are depression, bipolar disorder, dementia, schizophrenia, and anxiety disorders." (Source: National Mental Health Association)

tortured poor Paul long enough with my persistent questioning. Hoping to slip out without anyone noticing, I was clearly distressed by my surroundings. The whole world seemed different when I stepped outside. Trying to shake off how deeply disturbed I felt, I began pedaling home. I had attempted to identify with people outside my comfort zone and determined that it wasn't for me.

Fast forward three and a half years later to a very frosty January when the weather was cold, cold, cold. Subconsciously, I thought this delivery would be just like those depicted in the baby magazines, full of glowing anticipation, where everyone is wearing white and everyone is happy. Instead, I found myself in the hospital with my newborn son for his third admission in three weeks. Everything was indeed white, but everyone was not happy. This time, congestive heart failure had landed us in the nearest children's hospital about an hour from our home. That morning, Timmy had been diagnosed with a very serious heart condition not uncommonly found in babies with Down syndrome. According to his cardiologist, Timmy's case was a "worst-case scenario" for this particular cardiac anomaly. The hole in his heart was extremely large, about half the size of his little life-sustaining pump.

Still reeling from the news, we tried to settle into our assigned room that we were to share with three other families for the next five days. Needless to say, I was shocked at what I saw . . . and what I smelled . . . and what I heard. "Beep. Beep. Beep." Amidst the constant blipping of monitors was the incessant crying of babies, not simply because they were hungry, but because they were often being probed with needles. Usually, a nurse was trying to put in an intravenous line or draw blood for the afternoon lab report. The nine-month-old baby across the room had lived in there for much of her short life. A little girl who wandered down the hallway was literally missing half of her face. The sterile smells of hospital bedding replaced that gentle Ivory Snow scent I longed for at home. But this time, I couldn't walk out the door and hop on my bike and ride back to the safety of our house. This was my world now. The identification I had once ridden away from by choice was now mine by Providence.

Comfort and Identification

Most people are not immediately at ease with those who have disabilities—especially cognitive disabilities or mental illness. While today's generation of children has had greater exposure to individuals affected by disability, most adults still struggle with a fear factor when first learning to relate to people with disabilities. At times the fear is based on a stereotype that must be overcome. Sometimes it stems from the awkward feeling that arrives when we just don't know what to do or say. At times, we are confronted with the honest truth that we wrongly look at disability as an abnormal part of life in a normal world. In other instances, the discomfort comes from the vulnerable realization that disability is a condition that any of us can (and many of us will) personally encounter at some point in our lifetime—and that uncomfortable thought makes us want to run away.

There is also a societal component in that we live in a fragmented culture—one that is full of distinct lobbying groups. Typically, these groups communicate *at* each other but not *with* each other. To the degree that we passively absorb current postmodern cultural constructs about the impossibility of communication across different groups of people, we will fail even to attempt to connect with others whom we perceive to be different from ourselves. When we do this, we implicitly accept society's view of "community"— which is not a group of people bonded by *intentionality* but a group of people defined entirely by their *exclusivity*. For example, notice how language has changed in the last generation. We no longer refer to the "melting pot of America" to represent the cohesive bonding of this nation. Instead, "community" is a word used to define separate and distinct power groups. Listen carefully. You hear it on the news every day: the Hispanic Community, the Black Community, the Muslim Community, the Disability Community. When we focus on our differences, we tend to impart value—usually negative— to those differences. Instead of connecting with people affected by disability by choosing to stress our common humanity, we emphasize the differences to legitimize our desire to simply pursue our own agendas—those specific to our "community"—whatever they might be.

There is a common expression: *We're all in the same boat.* One doesn't have to experience much of life to recognize that this is an oversimplification of reality. A more accurate statement would be *same lake, different boat.* It reflects the truth that, as human beings, we share a common story, but the details of our experiences and our life circumstances may vary significantly. We are *essentially* the same but *experientially* different. However, the current societal emphasis goes far beyond this. Instead of seeing ourselves in the same lake, but in different boats, we tend to see ourselves in *different lakes entirely.* The result is that we end up feeling justified in simply seeking our own level of personal comfort in life—unaffected by the needs or desires of those around us.

Let's be honest. We all like comfort. One could even say that twenty-first century Americans are obsessed with it. Our cars, our furniture, our clothes, our computer keyboards—even our coffee cups are designed for ease of use. Just the right feel—a perfect fit. That's comfort in the material sense. Now, suppose someone says to you, "I just love my friends. I really *identify* with them." What are they likely referring to? It is highly probable that they are referring to a collection of people with whom their *comfort level* is high. To an outsider, it is a group where the commonality might be obvious across the individuals—consistent with society's version of community. But *The American Heritage Dictionary* definition of what it means to *identify* with another is much broader than this. It reads: "To associate or affiliate oneself closely with a person or group." This definition does not necessarily imply *comfort* or identification that is *easy*—just identification that is *purposeful*.

Biblical Identification

The Bible is replete with rich teaching about and examples of genuine identification. From Genesis to Revelation, the Scriptures demonstrate God's intentional identification with us. Ponder the depth of the word *Emmanuel*, which means "*God with us.*" From creation to the consummation of all things, God is committed to intentional identification with the creatures he designed in his image. According to Gerard Van Groningen, an Old Testament seminary professor, God's divine covenants constitute a "God-established, -maintained, and -implemented life-love bond."[1] God's covenants with his people throughout the ages are exemplary of the Emmanuel principle.

Consider the covenant of creation, which is God's implicit covenant with mankind made in the context of the design of humanity. The bond of life and love is deeply rooted in God's creation of man as his image-bearer. It is the relationship between God and man—not just in the simplistic sense that we usually think of the word *relationship*, but in the deeper sense of man's essence—his bearing of the divine image within himself—that binds man to God. Van Groningen continues, "This relationship is an essential aspect of God's covenant. The foundational idea of covenant is bond. God bound himself to mankind as he bound mankind to himself. It was a bond of life and love."[2]

Not only are we created for loving service to God in his kingdom, but we bear the image of the King himself within ourselves. Now, *that's* identification! If God, who, in all his splendor and transcendence can choose to be immanent to us, shouldn't we, who are clearly not transcendent, strive for association with our fellow human beings?

How do we know this is possible for us? We can be confident of our calling to identification because Jesus himself demonstrated it throughout his life. One of my favorite examples is in John's gospel account of Jesus' healing of the man who was born blind.

> As he went along, he saw a man blind from birth. His disciples asked him, "Rabbi, who sinned, this man or his parents, that he was born blind?"
>
> "Neither this man nor his parents sinned," said Jesus, "but this happened so that the work of God might be displayed in his life." (John 9:1–3)

The disciples emphasize a sense of otherness in the way they refer to "this man" and in the way they ask, "Who sinned?" Notice, however, that Jesus turns their question on its head and responds with a statement reflecting God's purposeful identification with the man's life: "This happened so that the work of God might be displayed in his life" (John 9:3). Jesus then proceeds to heal the man, but Jesus does not disengage from the man born blind at that point even though the man goes on his own way. The continuing account relays a subsequent squabble among the Pharisees, the man, and his family. Under a barrage of questioning, the healed man repeatedly recounts his miraculous encounter with the Christ, but the man is increasingly berated by those who do not want to accept it. Finally, the conflict ends with the Pharisees shouting at him, "You were steeped in sin at birth; how dare you lecture us!" (John 9:34). And they throw him out.

However, the best part of the story comes in the next verse. It reads, "Jesus heard that they had thrown him out, and when he found him . . ." (John 9:35). I love those words: "*when he found him.*" Jesus went looking for the man. He was interested in more than just his disability. He was invested in him as a person. Jesus then moves the relationship to another level and introduces himself as the Son of Man—bringing the relationship full circle back to a connection with God himself—the one who identified with the man born blind even in his creation, when the image of God was stamped within. That's powerful!

Biblical Application

So, from the profound reality of God's identification with us in our image-bearing and from Jesus' practical example, how do we make the jump to our own application? What motivates us to connect with others intentionally as God requires of us? Romans 12 gives a clue:

> For by the grace given me I say to every one of you: Do not think of yourselves more highly than you ought, but rather think of yourself with sober judgment, in accordance with the measure of faith God has given you. Just as each of us has one body with many members, and these members do not all have the same function, so in Christ we who are many form one body, and each member belongs to all the others. We have different gifts, according to the grace given us. (Rom. 12:3–6a)

The first thing that motivates us to identify with others is a proper perspective on ourselves. "Do not think of yourselves more highly than you ought" (Rom. 12:3). We must recognize that we all have needs—that is a normal part of life in an abnormal world. Our brokenness and neediness as humans is universal; how it manifests itself is variable. It is *same lake, different boat.* Connecting to others in a condescending way is not an option. Intentionally associating with others because we can truly identify with their human condition is essential.

Second, we will be motivated to identify with others when we realize that we rely on each other. "Just as each of us has one body with many members, and these members do not all have the same function, so in Christ we who are many form one body, and each member belongs to all the others" (Rom. 12:4–5). There is an interdependent unity that comes from diversity in the body of Christ. Everyone benefits when we choose intentional relationships with people of differing abilities. Notice that the model for mutual reliance in Christ's church is more intimate than *same lake, different boat*. It is *same body, different parts*.

Third, we need to celebrate the giftedness of those with whom we connect. "We have different gifts, according to the grace given us" (Rom. 12:6a). Because we are reliant on each other to bring completeness to the body of Christ, everyone's contribution is a gift in its own right. Note that our differing abilities are seen as positive and purposeful. There is genuine joy in celebrating the unique qualities that express God-given individuality in the context of unity.

Finally, "the grace given us" (Rom. 12:6a) is the ultimate basis for true person-to-person identification. In the covenant family, grace is the glue that binds us to each other—regardless of nationality, ability, gender, age, or any other defining characteristic. Those who have experienced God's grace firsthand know that our need for grace is universal. It is what allows us to relate to others, inside and outside of the body of Christ, with humility and compassion. Of course, identification can be costly and sometimes a little uncomfortable on our part, but grace was exceedingly costly and excruciatingly painful on God's part. Remember: Emmanuel—*God with us*. Doesn't that say it all?

Summary

When our son Freddy entered second grade, we were preparing to start Timmy in kindergarten at the same elementary school. Knowing that Timmy occasionally pulled embarrassing stunts in public, I was concerned that Freddy might feel self-conscious about sitting with Timmy on the school bus. So, one day I asked Freddy how he felt about the prospect of riding on the bus together. Looking at me in stunned amazement that I had even approached him with the question, Freddy replied indignantly, "I would be proud to sit with my brother."

How about you? Would you be proud to identify with your "brother" or "sister" who is disabled? Then follow Jesus' example—be intentional and go find them.

Personal Application Questions

1. How do you usually think about the concept of "identification"? Do you typically consider identification to be related to comfort, commonality, or intentionality?

2. What fears do you have about relating to people who have disabilities?

3. How does God's example of identification with us help you to overcome those fears?

4. What does it mean to say "same lake, different boat—we are all essentially the same but experientially different"?

5. Whom will you choose to identify with today?

3

On Respect: Common Grace, Special Needs

Honor one another above yourselves. —Romans 12:10b

Honestly, I think it was meant to be the community-pool version of a tidal wave. But what started out as the force behind a wall of water quickly turned into a full-fledged slap across the face. Suspended in time, the event unfolded like a super-slow-motion dramatic sequence in an action film. I saw the rage in his eyes and heard myself thinking *No . . . o . . . o . . . o . . . !!* but it was too late. Five-year-old Freddy—the protective older brother—unleashed his fury on two taunting girls in the shallow end of the pool. Timmy had been standing poolside, wonderfully excited about the prospect of going swimming. At age three, he sometimes expressed emotional overload by flapping his arms, opening his mouth, and blinking his eyes repeatedly. This day was no exception. Usually people noticed but, after a quick glance, continued on their way. However, this time two little girls decided that Timmy's behavior was entertaining and began to laugh, point, and imitate him with exaggerated movements. Apparently it was more than Freddy's justice-oriented personality could handle. He drew back his arm and swiftly administered the due penalty. Perhaps he was prompted by Proverbs 9:12b, which says, "*If you are a mocker, you alone will suffer,*" but somehow I don't think that is what went through his head.

Within seconds, our family was sitting on the grass near the pool deck while Freddy received his own share of compassionate justice for hitting two young ladies—albeit two very *rude* young ladies. Struggling with his first experience of public, intentional disrespect toward Timmy, Freddy experienced a very teachable moment. While his response to the mocking girls was inappropriate, Freddy had rightly recognized disrespect when he saw it. What is the basis of true respect? Do we recognize it when we see it? Do we know how to practice it?

Webster's Dictionary describes *respect* as "to feel or show honor or esteem for; to hold in high regard." Doesn't that definition clearly capture how every one of us longs to be treated? In popular culture today, the practice of demonstrating respect is becoming increasingly rare. At the same time, intrinsic to the fabric of our humanity is the need for respect, because respect is foundational to genuine relationships. What is the biblical warrant for this esteem we are to show each other in our interactions? The Scriptures show us that there are two "pillars of respect" that undergird our relationships. Those pillars are the image of God and grace.

The First Pillar: The Image of God

What do you first envision when you think of respect? Is it high regard for those in authority? Perhaps it is honor for the elderly. Maybe it is esteem for a person's noteworthy accomplishments or for their ability to persevere. The Bible indeed teaches that individuals in positions of authority, those who have seen many days, and people who live their lives in an admirable fashion are worthy of our respect. But there is something much deeper and inherently more central to the concept of respect, something that touches every human being. It is the reality that we are created in the image of God. The glory of God imprinted into the essence of man is absolutely central to the understanding of respect in relationships.

Jerram Barrs, Francis Schaeffer Scholar at Covenant Theological Seminary, put it this way:

> Scripture calls us to recognize that everyone we're ever going to meet is made in the image of God—and that means they're glorious. . . . That's to be our first response: to see the glory of a person . . . to first see their glory and their dignity as a person made in the image of God and to treasure all the things that are good and admirable and beautiful about the person as a person made in the image of God.[1]

Now, let's be honest. How many of us respond to even our closest family and friends this way? When was the last time you looked at your children and stood in awe of the glory of God within them? How about your spouse? When you are in a hurry to get to soccer practice and a cashier at McDonald's—a person with obvious developmental disabilities*—s-l-o-w-l-y

FIG. 1

The Pillars of Respect Support Relationships

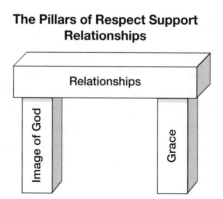

---

* "Developmental disabilities (DD) are severe, life-long disabilities attributable to mental and/or physical impairments, manifested before age 22. Developmental disabilities result in substantial limitations in three or more areas of major life activities." (Source: U.S. Administration on Developmental Disabilities) attempts to process your order and count out your change, do you first and foremost see the glory of God? If you are at a restaurant and a man with cerebral palsy* drools on his shirt at the table next to you, is your first realization one of wonder and honor?

Consider it this way: the image of God within each individual can be likened to a mirror that reflects God's glory, in part, to others. Unmarred at creation, what an incredible and awesome reflection that must have been! In a world now impacted by the fall, each person's mirror is cracked, yet all the pieces still remain. Consequently, the looking glass reflects a distorted view of God's glory—but it remains a partial mirror of him just the same. Our struggle enters in because we find it so much easier to identify the cracks in the mirror, and so we miss the image entirely. It takes a conscious effort for us to concentrate on the most fundamental blessing of creation—that we are all created in the image of God—and to gaze speechlessly at his goodness, truth, and beauty in others. Yet lives are radically transformed—ours and those around us—when we intentionally choose to focus on the image of God within.

The Second Pillar: Grace

Respectful relationships have to deal with both realities of life—the blessedness of creation and the brokenness of the fall. In our interactions with people, the blessedness of creation is found by discovering God's image within others. We need to search for his glory in each individual until we find it, and then we need to celebrate it! However, we also must acknowledge that the brokenness of the fall comes to bear heavily in our relationships, too. Personalities rub us the

* "Cerebral palsy is a term used to describe a group of chronic conditions affecting body movement and muscle coordination. It is caused by damage to one or more specific areas of the brain, usually occurring during fetal development; before, during, or shortly after birth; or during infancy." (Source: United Cerebral Palsy)

wrong way, people bring sinful behaviors to their dealings, or sometimes the sheer needs of others overwhelm us. How do we contend with that in each other? In the same way that God deals with us—with grace.

What exactly is grace? In Luke's gospel, there is a marvelous passage where Jesus is teaching in the synagogue. Reading from Isaiah, he proclaims:

> The Spirit of the Lord is on me,
>> because he has anointed me
>> to preach good news to the poor.
> He has sent me to proclaim freedom for the prisoners
>> and recovery of sight for the blind,
> to release the oppressed,
>> to proclaim the year of the Lord's favor. (Luke 4:18–19)

When you hear the words *poor*, *prisoner*, *blind*, and *oppressed*, what picture appears in your mind? Most likely, you think of someone else. And that someone else is a person whom you deem to be weaker than yourself. But when we truly understand grace, we realize that the poor, the prisoners, the blind, and the oppressed *are us*. We are the ones with desperate needs, and God, who is rich in grace, has met us in our need. He alone is the one operating from a position of strength. He is the one who is active in *our* lives—preaching, proclaiming, recovering, and releasing. The beauty of the gospel, if we truly understand it, is that each of us faces a complete barrier to participation in the kingdom of God due to the profoundly disabled condition of our hearts. The good news is that Christ's perfect sacrifice applied to us makes our full participation in the life of God a reality. We must come with "empty hands" depending on Christ alone to facilitate that life for us. Conference speaker Paige Benton once put it this way: "Not only *may* you come with empty hands, you actually *must* come with empty hands, because the essence of the gospel is grace."[2]

As a board member for a disability advocacy agency, I occasionally have the opportunity to visit local group homes to interview residents. On one occasion, I met with a fine young man who had significant physical and intellectual disabilities. His arms and legs flailed uncontrollably, and while I sensed he could understand my speech, I found his method of communication extremely difficult to interpret. After a brief conversation with him, I quietly asked a staff person at the home about the nature of his disability. She informed me that as a six-month-old infant this young man's head had been smashed into a wall by his father. Can you imagine anything more tragic than that? Such a crime demonstrates the brokenness of the fall in bold relief. Unable to work as a consequence of his disability, this individual is financially poor. Captive to the random, uncontrollable movements of his limbs, he knows the reality of being a prisoner to his body. Abused by his own father, he has firsthand knowledge of what it is like to know oppression. This young man is much more in touch with the reality of his condition than most of us are. He *knows* that he is poor, that he is a prisoner, and that he is oppressed. The question is, *do we know that we are*? In order to extend grace to others in relationships, we have to deeply understand our own need for it. You can't give grace if you haven't received it.

What does grace look like when it is manifest in a relationship? Because grace begins with perspective on our own neediness, grace-based relationships impart respect to others in our path. Whenever we encounter brokenness in others we do not judge it, but we meet it—just as God meets us. If we relate to those with significant needs, we are patient with them, because we realize that we also have great needs of our own, albeit different ones. At the times that our relationships are costly, we will quickly remember that God's establishing a relationship with us was infinitely costly to him. And that recollection of his grace empowers us to show grace to others.

Benefits of Respect-Based Relationships

There are great benefits in following God's calling to respectful interactions with others. Solidly building our relationships with others on the image of God and grace produces a *powerful message, perspective, proper motivation,* and *protection.*

The first benefit is the *powerful message* that our respect-based relationships deliver to others. When the image of God within is central to our understanding of humanity, it sends a powerful message about human value to the world around us. Our culture often measures personal value as a function of productivity. The degree to which we are able to contribute to society is the degree to which we are valued. In God's economy, however, human value is defined by the Creator himself through the imprint of his image in mankind. Others take notice, not merely when we say this is true, but when we live like it is true. Our actions ought to declare, "You are incredibly valuable!" to everyone we meet.

In the same way, the *powerful message* of the gospel is demonstrated when we respond to others in grace-based actions. Our competitive culture is uncomfortable with the concept of weakness. When people see us acknowledge our frailties and intentionally engage others in the areas of their brokenness, we live out the gospel of grace in powerful ways.

The second benefit comes in the form of *perspective.* Seeing the present reality of the image of God in each person gives us perspective on ourselves and others. Looking for the image of God within is an exercise in encouragement. When we look for the "good and admirable and beautiful,"[3] we focus on the positive, and we will impart encouragement to others in the process of doing that. Learning to see God's image helps us to keep our perspective by focusing on the potential in every person, rather than focusing on limitations. It also aids us in emphasizing what matters most—a person's dignity—and not their abilities or disabilities.

Grace is by definition a *perspective* builder too. It requires us to look inward before we extend outward. When we operate from the consciousness of having received grace, genuine humility and respect for others flows from us. Regardless of our relative abilities or disabilities, grace levels the playing field.

The third benefit of following God's pattern for respectful relationships is that we will have the *proper motivation* for engaging in the lives of others. Being involved in the lives of people touched by disability is a pro-life ministry in the broadest sense. When we truly value the sanctity of human life, we recognize that it requires upholding and promoting the image of God in each person—across the spectrum of life and in all the circumstances that life can bring. Being pro-life is about what we are *for*, not what we are *against*. It is a conception-to-grave commitment—an all-of-life involvement—that calls us to everyday action. The individual who provides support for a person with special needs is upholding the sanctity of human life—and so are the parents who promote the image of God in their "typical" children by lovingly raising them. We honor the image of God within when we serve a neighbor who has AIDS, when we meet the needs of our spouse with cancer, or when we care for a family member with dementia. The concept of the sanctity of human life is immense and broad, and it motivates us to engage others in God's name in whatever we do.

Likewise, grace offers the *proper motivation* for our involvement in the lives of others, whether they have needs similar to or different from our own. Have you ever been the recipient of someone else's duty-driven ministry? It isn't any fun! When grace is truly, personally grasped, our ministry to others will flow from a heart of gratitude. And gratitude is an inherently beautiful, respectful motivation for ministry.

Finally, the last benefit is one of *protection*. Being firmly grounded in the principle that human life—*all* human life— has value and dignity because we are created in the image of

God protects us from devaluation. We live in an age when human worth is frequently under assault. Some individuals in the field of bioethics are challenging the universal value of human life. Scientific advancements in embryonic stem-cell research and human cloning are raising grave and complex ethical questions that are often glossed over in the promise of pursuing miracle cures. While we operate in a culture where rights for persons with disabilities are currently greater than they have ever been, we are deceiving ourselves if we think those rights can never be rescinded. The rights that people with disabilities now enjoy have *not* emerged due to a cultural acceptance of human significance as bestowed by the Creator—they are legal rights that can be eradicated as quickly as they have been granted. It is altogether likely that when the elderly and the disabled become too costly or too cumbersome for society's taste, we will find ourselves facing increasingly horrific issues. If we are not willing to embrace individuals with special needs when the climate is easy, where will we be when the going gets tough? Who will stand in the gap? Declaring and living out the truth—that mankind has unique value because we are created in the image of God—is the ultimate form of protection from devaluation for the human race.

And how does grace afford *protection*? Grace makes it safe to minister to others because we are free to make mistakes. Imperfect people engaged in imperfect relationships will always yield imperfect results. Equipped by grace, we can take the risks of investing in and connecting with others, knowing that we will frequently fall short. And that is OK. I have a friend, Diane, who has cerebral palsy and uses a wheelchair. She is so gracious to me. Several times a year we go on adventures around town that require her to tolerate my highly limited wheelchair-driving skills! I have emptied her onto the sidewalk, forgotten to strap her into the correct seatbelts in the handicap-accessible van, and run her into doorframes. Of course, I don't do these things to her on purpose! I'm just not very adept at operating her mode of transportation. Because Diane practices exercising grace, however, we usually laugh our way through my incompetence, and I try again the next time.

Summary

Our lives always become richer when we follow God's pattern for living. Respectful relationships are possible when we discover the glory of God in others by focusing on his image within and when we extend the grace of God to others because we have experienced it ourselves.

Oh! Before I forget, in case you're wondering what advice I gave to Freddy at poolside, it was basically this: "It is not our job to punish people for their disrespectful attitudes toward Timmy. It is our job to educate them and show them the way by our example." Then we walked over to the pool together and had a lovely conversation with two young ladies. It was just the first conversation of many others like it.

Personal Application Questions

1. Prior to reading this chapter, how would you have defined *respect*? Now that you have read it, how would you describe it?

2. Are your relationships inherently respectful? Why or why not? How could you improve in this area?

3. In what ways do you need to learn to focus on the image of God in others, gazing at the "goodness, truth, and beauty" in those around you?

4. How deeply has God's grace gripped your life? In practical terms, how does grace manifest itself in your closest relationships?

4

On Relentlessness: Dante's Circles of Disability

Disability is not like cancer. You can't get to the other side of it. —Anonymous

Differences without difficulty. That's how I explained it. The essential question posed to me was, "Is there any room in creation, before the fall, for differences in abilities among people?" Absolutely. Differences without difficulty. The reality of experiencing disability as a *normal* part of life in an *abnormal* world is that disability brings difficulty. And one of the most challenging aspects of disability is the relentlessness of it. It just doesn't quit. You don't beat it. One cannot escape it. All of us can identify with relentlessness at some level. Have you ever tried to clean up toys after a toddler? How about keeping the outside of your car clean during a particularly messy winter? Many of the tasks we face in life are relentless: doing laundry, commuting to work, grocery-shopping, cooking, conducting auto maintenance, exercising, paying bills, and so on. Repetitive challenges can offer character-building opportunities in life. Yet the level of frustration we experience is often a function of *how we engage* the relentlessness in our lives.

As a junior at Western Maryland College, I took a course in continental literature. In that class we read Dante's

Inferno. The imagery of that portion of *The Divine Comedy* vividly remains with me. Throughout the poem, the concept of eternal torment is depicted as containing nine concentric circles. Each one involves an increasingly unpleasant, repetitive process that, almost upon completion, is entirely undone only to be repeated perpetually. A particularly memorable example is the tale of a man rolling an extremely heavy rock up a very steep hill. Almost at the top, he loses control of the rock, it rolls back down the hill, and he is destined to resume the exercise. Quite a picture of relentlessness! Have you ever felt that way about aspects of your life? What are the challenges that you face over and over again?

The behavioral component of Down syndrome is what usually brings Dante to visit at our home. Recounting the tales afterward typically incites laughter, but they are almost always exasperating events when they occur. When Timmy was five years old we had a notably memorable Dante's circles experience of behavioral relentlessness. It all began with an innocent activity on my part. I had taken a shower. While drying off, I still heard water running. Slowly turning the sentence over in my head I thought, *Funny, I . . . wonder . . . where . . . THERE'S . . . WATER RUNNING!* and I darted down the hallway to find Timmy. As I entered the laundry room, he was perched on top of the washing machine. Having put all the clean laundry from the dryer into the utility sink, he had then turned the faucets on full blast! Of course, the laundry clogged the sink and the water was cascading—and I mean *cascading*—over the lip of the sink and onto the floor. After turning off the water, sternly insisting that Timmy remain on top of the washer where I could see him, and tossing the soaked laundry out onto the deck, I began the frustrating process of mopping up the mess.

While attempting to remove the sea of water, I realized that there were holes in the floor where the sink pipes enter the basement. I asked seven-year-old Freddy to run down to the basement to see if water was leaking into the storage room below. With great intensity he came scrambling back up the stairs screaming: "There's water *everywhere!*" Knowing his tendency toward exaggeration, I asked him calmly, "Come on, Freddy. What's it really like?" to which he blurted out again, "There's water *everywhere!*" He was right. There was sopping insulation hanging from the ceiling and a standing puddle of water about twenty feet in diameter. Many of the items in our storage room were soaked. It took hours to clean up—in fact, the task was so immense that I called my husband Fred at work and asked him to come home and help me (which he did). I soon realized that the water had also run under the wall into the family room. The carpet was drenched, so we had to move all the books, bookshelves, and filing cabinets to dry and then clean the saturated rug.

The following day brought new excitement. We had recently acquired an adorable Bernese mountain dog puppy named Belle. Upon walking into the laundry room, I was privileged to see Belle's hind legs disappearing into the washing machine, compliments of Mr. Timmy. In disbelief I asked him, "What are you doing?" to which he replied, "I put her in. I turn it on." Exasperated, I replied firmly, "We don't *ever* put the dog into the washing machine, and if we do, we *never* turn it on!" Have you ever attempted to get a Bernese mountain dog out from around the agitator of a washer?

That evening, while making dinner, I took my eyes off Timmy for about five minutes. Five minutes was apparently too long. Our next-door neighbor found him down the road on the next street over, galloping his stick pony on the yellow line. When asked where he was going, Tim the cowboy replied, "To get the mail." Pony Express, I guess. Timmy enjoyed his ride home in the neighbor's Jeep Wrangler—very fitting with his theme at that moment. At this point, my anxiety level seemed to be rising in direct proportion to Timmy's level of enjoyment with the whole experience.

Soon thereafter, I was on the phone with a friend. Because Timmy had been in the habit of letting the puppy out of her crate, I had put a small padlock on it. While I was talking, Timmy found the keys and tossed them inside the dog crate. Belle quickly began to eat them. In disbelief, I squeezed my arm through the bars, only to find the keys millimeters out of my reach. After straining to reach them, I finally got the keys from the dog. That's when I realized that my arm was stuck—*really stuck*—between the bars. "TIMMY!" I eventually freed my arm only to realize that, all along, the dog crate had a tray that would have easily slid out. Oh well—sometimes it is difficult to think rationally when one is under stress.

The rampage of activity continued with two more floodings of the basement via highly creative methods. Timmy also managed to escape from a friend's supervision and embark on a neighborhood adventure that included visiting *inside* the home of unsuspecting strangers. The final event was a Houdini-like disappearance trick that Timmy executed for his father's entertainment and enjoyment. After searching for him frantically, Fred finally found Timmy —*in the clothes dryer.*

At times, relentless difficulties are something that we can laugh about when the intensity has ebbed. Often, though, there is nothing funny about them—during or afterward. For some families touched by disability, relentlessness comes in the form of providing decades of personal care, or heart-wrenching struggles with communication, aggression, or self-injury on the part of the individual with special needs. Maybe it arrives in the form of endless hospitalizations, lack of access to transportation, joblessness, social isolation, or any of a myriad of other issues.

Helen Featherstone, in her book *A Difference in the Family,* says that, for families affected by disability, "differences differ only in degree from those of other families."[1] Every family faces significant challenges in living and in raising a family. Every family has its own encounters with Dante's circles, but families affected by disability will find it to be more so—often *much more so*. And therein lies the potential danger. We need to recognize that three responses to relentlessness are available to each of us. The first one is to develop a victim mentality. The second is to attack it with an "I will beat this" attitude. The third is to engage reality with a perspective that is honest and God-reliant. Which one will we choose, and how will that impact how we live?

A Biblical Example

In the Scriptures, there are wonderful models of perseverance in the face of the mundane, the repetitive, or the relentless. Particularly stunning is the life of Joseph. His story is found in Genesis, beginning in chapter 37. In a nutshell, the story of Joseph tells us that he was betrayed and sold into slavery by his brothers, owned by the powerful man Potiphar, falsely accused of sexual assault by Potiphar's wife, imprisoned for years, forgotten by his friends, and then—ultimately used by God to save more than one nation.

When reading through these chapters in Genesis, one is struck by the parallels between Joseph's life and the life of a family affected by disability today. Of course there's not a perfect correlation, but there are some interesting parallels. What are they?

First, Joseph found himself thrust into a difficulty not of his own choosing. In fact, Joseph found himself thrust into *many* difficulties he would not have chosen. Betrayal. Slavery. Imprisonment. Abandonment. Disability is similar—it is a difficulty that no one seeks out. I have yet to meet anyone who wakes up in the morning, stretches, and says, "Say, I think I'll go out and acquire a disability today." Disability finds us; we don't find it.

Second, Joseph took a stand for righteousness and, as a result, found himself trapped in difficult circumstances. Joseph was imprisoned because he refused to succumb to the seductive advances of Potiphar's wife. As a reward for his stand for purity and his subsequent attempt to flee from her presence, she falsely accused him of rape. As Christians in today's culture, we may find ourselves in a similar dilemma with regard to abortion or euthanasia. For many of us, our convictions regarding the sanctity of human life have caused us to stand with Joseph and declare, "How then could I do such a wicked thing and sin against God?" (Gen. 39:9). So we flee from the presence of evil, and as a result of standing for righteousness, we may find ourselves in a challenging situation, caring for a child or adult family member with significant disabilities.

Third, Joseph was forgotten by those who knew of both his innocence and his integrity—even though they had benefited from his ministry. When Joseph was in prison, he continued to live a life of integrity. The Scriptures tell us that "the LORD . . . granted him favor in the eyes of the prison warden . . . and gave him success in whatever he did" (Gen. 39:21, 23b). When God led him to interpret the dreams of the chief baker and the chief cup bearer, both predictions came true exactly as Joseph had indicated. The chief baker was executed, and the chief cup bearer was restored to his job with Pharaoh. But the narrative tells us, "The chief cup bearer, however, did not remember Joseph; he forgot him" (Gen. 40:23). Does this ever happen in the church? Have you ever sensed that while lip service is given to the sanctity of human life, those who actually relentlessly uphold it in their daily lives are forgotten? Often, families affected by disability have ministered faithfully in their own Christian community, yet are not remembered—or supported—by those around them.

Fourth, Joseph was not restored to the land of Canaan until after his death. He lived out his life in Egypt. As Christians we believe that, someday, there will be the restoration of all things. One of the mysteries of the kingdom of God is what theologians call the "already-not-yet"—it is here in part, but will not be here in complete fullness until we reach glory. Disability, as just one of the more visible expressions of human brokenness, is therefore part of the already-not-yet-ness of the kingdom of God. It is a dimension of life where we can make an impact and bring some restorative power, but the fullness of that restoration—as with all of us—will not be known in this lifetime. Joseph, too, knew the reality of an already-not-yet existence. God used him in mighty and restorative ways in Egypt, but it was in Egypt that he lived out all his days.

Three Possible Responses to Relentlessness

Just as Joseph chose between options in responding to relentlessness, so must we. How might Joseph's story have unfolded differently had he chosen the lesser possibilities? And how might our lives change in a similar way?

Option 1: The Victim Mentality

What if the story of Joseph had been written by Albert Camus, the famous existentialist writer? If Camus refashioned the story, Joseph would have pondered his fate, despaired in the hopelessness of his situation, renounced God, and then died after a futile, meaningless existence. How distressing. Perhaps you've met families who are "Camusian" in their approach to life. They are victims to the core. *Sometimes you just draw the short straw. Life stinks.* In their minds the world owes them, you owe them, and God owes them, and there will be no peace until the perceived debt has been paid.

Option 2: The "I Will Beat This" Attitude

If the story of Joseph had been authored by a Hollywood screenwriter, Joseph would have gladly slept with Potiphar's wife upon the first opportunity. If he had ended up in prison, there would have been a stupendous *Escape from Alcatraz*-type breakout, jointly executed by Joseph, the chief baker, and the chief cup bearer. This trio would have eliminated Pharaoh and his entire army *Rambo*-style. Next, they would have journeyed to Canaan to engage Joseph's brothers with a vindictive vengeance. Have you ever met families like this? They are those who, in dealing with special needs, try to break free of them by blasting away at disability and everything in its path. In their thinking, disability *is* like cancer. One *can* get to the other side of it, and they will, regardless of the price.

What do these two extreme alternatives have in common? It is this: whether victim in mentality or victor in attitude, the initial crisis or tragedy becomes the central focus of that family's existence. *The difficulty defines all of life.*

Option 3: Engage Reality with a God-Reliant Perspective

How was Joseph's choice different from the other options, and what can we learn from his example? Joseph was not a victim or a victor; he *engaged his reality with a God-reliant perspective.* What exactly does that mean? It means that he had the courage to face honestly whatever life brought because his life was God-focused and not difficulty-focused. Look at the attributes of God's character mentioned throughout the account of Joseph. The story refers to God's presence, his holiness, his kindness, and his providence. Time and again we see that Joseph's faith was focused on his God: that he is who he says he is, and that he will do what he says he will do. It was Joseph's God-reliant existence that allowed him to engage his reality with enhanced perspective. What perspective did a God-focus provide for Joseph?

First, it provided a perspective on personal power. Power is big in American culture—*really* big. And Egyptian culture was probably no different. So, it is amazing to consider Joseph's story at the point where the chief cup bearer finally did indeed remember him, and Joseph was released from the prison to interpret Pharaoh's dream. At this juncture, Joseph had already been through significant difficulties. He had been betrayed by his brothers, imprisoned on false charges, and forgotten for two years after the chief cup bearer was released. Wouldn't you have felt like it was time to take things into your own hands? Joseph was finally out of prison, and now he was standing before Pharaoh. Pharaoh addressed Joseph, saying, "I had a dream, and no one can interpret it. But I have heard it said of you that when you hear a dream, you can interpret it" (Gen. 41:15). This was his window of opportunity, and Joseph knew it. This was his passport to freedom. What would you do? Wouldn't you start to preen your feathers a bit and in false modesty say, "Well, it's a gift, you know!" But that's not at all how Joseph responded. This is what he replied: "I cannot do it. . . ." *What*? What is Joseph *doing*? Then he went on: "But God will give Pharaoh the answer he desires" (Gen. 41:16). That's incredible. Joseph had a perspective on personal power that can come only from a God-reliant life.

The second way that a God-focused life brought perspective to Joseph was in his penchant for the positive. In the animated movie *Shrek*, one of the main characters is a little donkey who is "way stressed out." Every time there is a crisis or an obstacle he becomes filled with anxiety, talking rapidly and incessantly to anyone who will listen to his distress. Was Joseph like this little donkey? When he revealed Pharaoh's dream and recognized the severity of the prophecy, did he run around the room hysterically crying, "We're all gonna DIE!"? No. Joseph's focus on the character of God—that God is great, *and* God is good—allowed him to be positive and solution-oriented in his approach to life. A penchant for the positive resulted in the saving of many lives (Gen. 50:20) by focusing on the food that could be stored to prepare for the approaching famine, and not focusing exclusively on the famine itself.

The third type of perspective that a God-focused life provided Joseph was a progressive sense of purpose. Did Joseph know what God ultimately had in store for him at the time he was sold into slavery? Nothing in the biblical account supports that idea. But apparently—and this was probably not without struggle—Joseph believed in God's providential working in his life. Joseph's progressive sense of purpose grew out of faith in God's providence. This helped him persevere through the unfolding of God's plan for his life. I love what he said upon revealing himself to his brothers near the end of the story:

> And now, do not be distressed and do not be angry with yourselves for selling me here, because it was to save lives that God sent me ahead of you. For two years now there has been a famine in the land, and for the next five years there will not be plowing and reaping. But God sent me ahead of you to preserve for you a remnant on earth and to save your lives by a great deliverance.
>
> So, then, it was not you who sent me here, but God. (Gen. 45:5–8)

A fourth area where Joseph gained perspective from his God-focused living was on the topic of pain. Nobody likes the pain of heartache and disappointment. Human beings put a tremendous amount of energy into pain avoidance. Sometimes that is a healthy thing—such as when it keeps us from getting sunburned or from driving so fast that we hurt ourselves in a car accident. But excessive pain avoidance can also make us neurotic. Joseph had a balanced perspective on pain because his heartache was not the central focus of his life. However, Joseph was also up front about his personal pain. He did not smooth over it, nor did he wallow in it—he engaged it with honesty and dependence on his God. This is demonstrated when the account says, "The second son he named Ephraim, and said, 'It is because God has made me fruitful in the land of my suffering'" (Gen. 41:52b). Notice his honesty and his God-reliance. He acknowledges both his suffering and his fruitfulness and that God is the source of his blessing in the midst of trouble.

Finally, Joseph had a proper perspective on the role of people in his life. Notice that Joseph's God-centered focus did not preclude his asking for assistance from others. After Joseph revealed the dream of the chief cup bearer, he said to him: "But when all goes well with you, remember me and show me kindness; mention me to Pharaoh and get me out of this prison" (Gen. 40:14). Joseph was not afraid to ask for help. Yet Joseph was not demanding. How can we tell? The account informs us when we see Joseph's reaction upon being released from prison. If Joseph's comments after the revelation of the dream had not been an earnest request but a demand, he would have exhibited an incredibly negative attitude toward the chief cup bearer upon his release—and it would likely have been included in the narrative. Instead, Joseph's God-reliance allowed him to have a proper perspective of people. He could be vulnerable and ask for help, but he knew his ultimate Helper was God himself.

Summary

So, where does all of this take us? Interestingly, this story about a famous Hebrew ultimately takes us to the book of Hebrews in the New Testament. Chapter 11 of Hebrews is sometimes referred to as the Faith Hall of Fame. Predictably, Joseph is mentioned in it. Joseph's example, among many others, is a wonderful backdrop to these verses of encouragement that follow:

> Therefore, since we are surrounded by such a great cloud of witnesses, let us throw off everything that hinders and the sin that so easily entangles, and let us run with perseverance

> the race marked out for us. Let us fix our eyes on Jesus,
> the author and perfecter of our faith. . . . (Heb. 12:1–2a)

Whether dealing with relentlessness in your own life or relentlessness in the lives of families you know who are affected by disability, ponder this question: "What is 'everything that hinders and the sin that so easily entangles'?" Whatever the answer in your situation, take heart and follow Joseph's example. Whether you are coming alongside of a family affected by disability or you are facing the mundane, repetitive, or relentless aspects of your own life, the solution is the same. We each need to ask God to help us evaluate our hearts and to provide perspective through a God-focused life—fixing our eyes on Jesus, the author and perfecter of our faith—that we may run with perseverance the race marked out *for us.*

Personal Application Questions

1. What is your personal inclination—to be difficulty-focused or God-focused?

2. Are there times when you think and behave like a victim—as if Camus rather than God were the author of your story? Can you think of others in your life who tend to respond to relentlessness in this way?

3. Are there times when you spend endless amounts of energy trying to engage difficulty in your life, as if "you will beat this"—Hollywood-style? Do you know others in your life who tend to respond to relentlessness in this way?

4. Have you vacillated between either of these extremes, rather than engaging your reality with God's perspective—honestly and courageously facing whatever life brings because you are God-focused instead of difficulty-focused?

5. Do you, or does someone you know, need to regain a godly perspective on some issues?

- Are you secretly preoccupied with personal power? How does this preoccupation manifest itself?
- Maybe you've lost your penchant for the positive, or you've never been able to find it in the first place! Is your focus on the famine and you've lost sight of God's solution and provision in the middle of it?
- Perhaps you've wandered from a sense of purpose and can no longer see any good in your situation. Have you forgotten about God's providence in your life?
- Did you stop letting yourself feel the pain a long time ago—or maybe that's all you feel—and either way, the result has been to lose out on the fullness of life?
- Do you struggle with people who "just don't get it" when it comes to understanding the challenges in your life? Do you need help but have become too proud to ask or too burned to try again? Have you forgotten who your ultimate Helper is?

5

On Restoration: Thy Kingdom Come

To spread the Kingdom of God is more than simply winning people to Christ. It is also working for the healing of persons, families, relationships and nations; it is doing deeds of mercy and justice. —Timothy J. Keller

It had been almost a year since we received the news—the good news about the kingdom. The Magic Kingdom, that is. The announcement came from a generous Philadelphia-based foundation that provides free trips to Disney World for families touched by a variety of disabilities and illnesses. We were awarded such a trip and decided to make it a surprise for our boys. On the day that we were set to leave we gave them a poem that included hints—requiring Freddy and Timmy to dash around the house, find the clues, and put the pieces of the puzzle together. When they unraveled the mystery, their expressions were priceless! The joy, the disbelief, the excitement, the anticipation! So many emotions jam-packed into such a brief moment!

It truly was a vacation to remember. The trip included free airfare and free accommodations in a private cottage, complete with unlimited access to a pool, playground, and mini-golf course. Spending money and a free rental car were also included, plus Disney theme-park tickets for the whole family for four days. Oh, and yes, special passes to go to the front of the line on rides—even on the weekend in the summer. Does it get any better than that? With the exception of a few travel complications, we thoroughly enjoyed our activities and each other for five wonderfully memorable days. It was a marvelous experience for which we will always be deeply grateful. And yet, it too was a brief moment. Come and gone.

Restoration or Compensation

During our Magic Kingdom adventure, my husband and I occasionally discussed our reactions to being the recipients of such generosity. It took tremendous grace to receive a gift of such magnificent proportions. We had to admit that we did not feel worthy of the generosity extended to us. What was the motivation for such an outpouring of kindness on the part of strangers? Not wanting to waste a moment of the experience, we did not linger on the question. Reflecting on that curiosity in retrospect, however, I have to wonder this: Is the purpose of such an expression primarily found in an attempt to provide "restoration" or "compensation"? My suspicion is that it is often the latter.

In American society, we have come to expect to be compensated for our difficulties in life. Having lost our moorings spiritually, we no longer have a context for suffering or struggle in a culture that denies not only the sovereignty but the very existence of Almighty God. Our court system has become overburdened with lawsuits by those seeking compensation for undesirable events in their lives, even if malice or neglect were not contributing factors. Someone has to pay. Sometimes we can fall into the trap of viewing disability in a similar way. Instead of seeing it as a normal part of life in an abnormal world, it can be viewed as an unlucky tragedy that requires some type of compensation. Have you ever caught yourself thinking this way when you see the Special Olympics contribution box on the counter of your local convenience store?

A Different Kind of Kingdom

There is, however, a kingdom to be experienced whose substance is not "magical" or "come and gone." Nor is it tied to the "*compensation* of all things." Instead, it is "real" and "already, not yet." And it promotes the "*restoration* of all things." It is a partially present reality with a future, consummating hope—it is the kingdom of God. As Tim Keller states in his book *Ministries of Mercy: The Call of the Jericho Road,*

> Christ came to bring the kingdom of God back to earth. The kingdom is *the power of the king.* Thus the kingdom of God is the renewal of the whole world through the entrance of supernatural forces. As things are brought back under Christ's rule and authority, they are restored to health, beauty, and freedom.[1]

Keller clarifies that "the healing kingship of Christ will extend to all of life and nature. The blessedness of the kingdom is radical and all-embracing (Matt. 5:3–10). . . . The kingdom of God is the means for the renewal of the entire world in all the dimensions of life."[2] One cannot imagine a more comprehensive restoration than what is promised through the kingdom of God: all of life redeemed. The kingdom is here in part—right now. And the kingdom is coming in complete fullness—in the future.

My Kingdom Come vs. Thy Kingdom Come

Jesus spoke about the kingdom of God more frequently than about any other subject. It is the unifying theme of the four gospels. Yet it seems that we often have trouble defining it or squirm at explaining how it translates into our daily lives. Perhaps that is because of the challenging concept of the "already-not-yet-ness" of the kingdom. But could it be due to our reluctance to integrate the two realities of the kingdom into our lives? In his classic book entitled *The Coming of the Kingdom*, Herman Ridderbos states, "At first sight the gospel of the kingdom of heaven consists of two parts which together form an unbreakable unity. The first part is related to the *gift*, the *salvation*, given in the gospel; the other part is related to the *demand*, the *command* in which it is expressed."[3] Could it be that we want the gift without the demand? Do we want the benefits of the kingdom without bending the knee to the King in all areas of life? Consider the following observation by Chuck Colson:

> Because of the nature of the King and the price He paid for His Kingdom, much is required of its citizens, and Jesus made these demands of the Kingdom clear. . . . Through the centuries, however, many of His followers have watered down His teaching, stripped away His demands for the building of a righteous society, and preached an insipid religion concerned with only personal benefits. This distorted view portrays Christianity not as a powerful source of spiritual rebirth and the mediating force for justice, mercy, and love in the world, but as the ultimate self-fulfillment plan. The gospel is not a release for the captives, but confidence for the shy. It is the spiritual equivalent of racy sports cars, designer clothes, and Gordon's Gin—a commodity to help one get more out of life.[4]

What are these demands of the kingdom? Once we have become *identified* with the kingdom of God through utter dependence on Christ alone for salvation, we have the privilege and responsibility of being *instruments* of the kingdom of God—vehicles through whom the loving power of the King flows into the lives of those around us through our voluntary, obedient service. God's love displays its power of restoration in and through the powerful, active presence of the Holy Spirit in our lives.

What does this mean in practical terms? One way of looking at how God delivers his restorative power is through *healing*, *help*, and *hope*. Think about the "already-not-yet-ness" of the kingdom being reflected along a spectrum of expressions of restoration. *Healing* is the fullest and most present expression of restoration, *hope* is the most future-oriented expression, and *help* is in the continuum in between.

Restoration through Healing

Bringing up the subject of healing in Christian circles is always risky business. Almost immediately, people polarize into dramatically different, theologically entrenched positions from which they are generally unmovable. Countless volumes have been written about healing, and this book is not intended to be one of them. However, when one discusses restoration it is impossible to avoid discussing healing—because that is precisely what restoration is ultimately about—the healing of brokenness. What we so often seem to forget, though, is the need to go back to creation and the fall to recall how universal and permeating the presence of brokenness is. As explained in chapter 1, each of us experiences some mix of the blessedness of creation and the brokenness of the fall. We participate in this combination in every aspect of life—the spiritual, physical, intellectual, psychological, social, and emotional. The struggle we have when we discuss healing is that we tend to isolate it to the realm of the physical, ignoring all the other dimensions. Upon isolating it to the realm of the physical, we tend to insist that it is either utterly unavailable in this lifetime or entirely available upon demand. Then the theological tug-of-war begins. We are uncomfortable at the thought of living with the tension of something in between: the already-not-yet-ness of the kingdom of God.

Consider the words of Francis Schaeffer from *The God Who Is There*:

> The Bible does not promise us perfection in this life, except in the area of justification. It does not promise us in this life perfection morally, physically, psychologically or sociologically. There are to be moral victories and growth, but that is different from perfection. . . . There can be physical healing, but that does not mean that the one healed is then a perfect physical specimen. The day Lazarus was raised from the dead he may have had a headache, and certainly one day he died again. People can be wonderfully helped psychologically, but that does not mean that they will then be totally integrated personalities. The Christian position is understanding that on this side of the resurrection the *call* is to perfection, and yet at the same time not to smash and destroy what we cannot bring again to life—just simply because it is less than the perfections that we romantically build in our thinking.[5]

Being instruments of the kingdom of God in this world means yielding to the agenda of the King, not following our own romantic notions of what that should look like. "A person can sow the seed, but the kingdom itself is God's deed."[6] Our obligation is to *obedience*; God is responsible for the *outcomes*. If "the kingdom of God is the renewal of the entire universe through the healing hands of the King,"[7] how does his healing power flow into the lives of those around us?

First of all, we can be instruments of healing through *prayer.* "The prayer of a righteous man is powerful and effective" (James 5:16b). Prayer is an act of dependence that recognizes that God himself is the only source of true healing and the only Deliverer in every dimension of life. Prayer is always the starting point because it reminds us again and again that God's sovereign, good, and perfect will is accomplished not only through us at times, but also in spite of us.

Second, we can be instruments of healing through *practice*. In the realm of physical healing, this practice may take the form of advancing curative research or providing medical care. For two years in a row, our pastor's daughter Katie won awards in county-wide and international science fair competitions for her research into the causes and treatment of multiple sclerosis (MS).* Motivated by watching her grandmother's courage and faith in the face of having lived with MS for more than fifty years, Katie chose to become a vehicle for the "healing hands of the King" through her research project. At the same time she brought honor to the King through the exemplary quality of the work that she offered.

Other types of healing can take place in practice through ministries that promote justice. Brokenness occurs in social systems and relationships too. We are instruments of the kingdom when we help to set right that which is unjust. "Is not this the kind of fasting I have chosen: to loose the chains of injustice and untie the cords of the yoke, to set the oppressed free and break from every yoke?" (Isa. 58:6). Kingdom work includes the work of advocacy. We are called to be a voice for those who are powerless—through inability or injustice—to be heard on their own. Even now there are remarkable court cases being litigated around the globe over "wrongful life" where parents are suing medical providers for supplying medical care that allowed their disabled child to *live*. Such action would have been unthinkable even a generation ago. When Christians confront such injustice on behalf of infants with disabilities—and the chains are loosed—the coming of the kingdom is felt.

Restoration through Help

Recall that along the spectrum of restoration, healing is the most presently experienced reality of the coming of the

---

* "Multiple sclerosis is a chronic, unpredictable neurological disease that affects the central nervous system." (Source: National Multiple Sclerosis Society)

kingdom. Healing implies a *reversal* of circumstances. But when reversal is not experienced, does that mean that the kingdom is not present even in part? When the power of the King is not felt through *healing*, it is still found through *help*. While *healing* implies restoration through *reversal*, *help* implies restoration through *assistance*. In practical terms, help is what stems the tide of a free fall into despair that can be experienced through brokenness. While help may not reverse the circumstances experienced, it can break the downward spiral of negativity that we all experience when faced with daunting challenges. By coming alongside those experiencing difficulty, help creates a place of safe reliance.

When Timmy was about four months old, the occasion of our ninth wedding anniversary came about. We were so disoriented by life events then that I'm not sure if we thought we'd been married for nine years or ninety. In the four short months since Timmy's birth, he had been hospitalized for jaundice, pneumonia, congestive heart failure, and bacterial spinal meningitis. Surviving the meningitis by the sheer providential grace of God that had placed us at a cardiology checkup *in the hospital* on the morning that the illness struck, we were still reeling from weeks of watching his little body suffer the awful effects of that devastating disease. Celebrating our anniversary wasn't a particularly high priority, and we probably didn't have the resources at our disposal to make such a celebration a reality even if it had crossed our minds.

Our closest friends, Roger and Patty, however, knew what we needed. They invited us over for dinner on our anniversary, offering to celebrate with us. When we arrived at the door with the boys in our arms, they scooped them up and ushered us inside. Set with fine china, flowers, and beautiful linens was a table for two. Just two. And in the oven was a completely prepared steak dinner, already masterfully arranged on warmed plates. Before we could grasp what was occurring, Roger and Patty bolted out the door with our children and theirs in tow, off to our house to spend the evening while we relished some much-needed time alone. Our friends could not heal the effects of our traumatized hearts through reversing events, but they still knew that they could bring the loving restorative power of the King through providing help. By relying on their assistance with the care of our children, and accepting the free grace of the gift they were offering, we experienced a marvelous and memorable act of restoration in our lives.

Restoration through Hope

If *healing* is the closest form of the already-ness of the coming of the kingdom of God, and if *help* moves farther down the spectrum toward the not-yet-ness of the kingdom of God, then *hope* points us most clearly to the ultimate consummation of the kingdom of God in the future. *Healing* implies *reversal,* *help* implies *assistance,* and *hope* implies *reminding.* Remember that the coming of the kingdom is also a future event. It is the looking forward to the consummation of all things. When healing is not in the will of God's providence, and help is not enough—and it never will be in this lifetime—then hope is always a present reality.

> Then I saw a new heaven and a new earth, for the first heaven and the first earth had passed away, and there was no longer any sea. I saw the Holy City, the new Jerusalem, coming down out of heaven from God, prepared as a bride beautifully dressed for her husband. And I heard a loud voice from the throne saying, "Now the dwelling of God is with men, and he will live with them. They will be his people, and God himself will be with them and be their God. He will wipe away every tear from their eyes. There will be no more death or mourning or crying or pain, for the old order of things has passed away."
>
> He who was seated on the throne said, "I am making everything new!" Then he said, "Write this down, for these words are trustworthy and true." (Rev. 21:1–5)

Words that are trustworthy and true—like the character of the King himself—are what give us restoration through hope.

Ben was an amazing young man who exemplified great hope even in the midst of overwhelming circumstances. Ben lived as a typical preschooler until the age of four, but his life and the life of his family were changed forever by the discovery of a brain tumor. After years of unsuccessful treatments and increasing levels of disability—eventually surviving for two years paralyzed and on a ventilator—it became clear that healing was not going to occur in this lifetime. While reliance on years of help from the body of Christ assisted the family to experience God's restorative power, in the end, Ben died at age thirteen. While attending his funeral, I was overcome with sadness for his family and all that they had suffered over the course of a decade. After greeting them in the receiving line— and feeling more encouraged by their presence than I am sure they felt by mine—I escaped to another room where I dissolved into tears. As I emerged, Keith—an adult friend of mine who has Down syndrome—greeted me. He observed that I had been crying, and he was very, very intentional about speaking to me. He started out with his predictable, traditional greeting, "Do you love Jesus?" I was not in the mood for this conversation. "Ben loved Jesus," Keith said reflectively. Nodding patronizingly, I mumbled something in response to him. "And Ben is with Jesus!" Keith exclaimed. "And he grew up!" Keith continued. Uh-huh. Not being willing to be dismissed so lightly, he became very animated—strutting around the narthex and motioning with his hands, "And he can walk!" Finally, getting directly in front of my face, Keith cried, "And he can *see* Him!!" He got my attention. I started listening to what Keith was saying and looked at the joy on his face. Ben had had hope. Keith understood the same hope. And Keith, my teacher, knew that I needed to be reminded of it too. I experienced restoration through an instrument of the King that day when Keith reminded me to "hold unswervingly to the hope we profess, for he who promised is faithful" (Heb. 10:23).

Summary

Are you an instrument of the kingdom of God, bringing healing, help, and hope to those around you who are experiencing some form of brokenness in their lives? Are you willing to accept the coming of the kingdom into your life when you are blessed to be the recipient of restoration in its various forms?

"Thy Kingdom come, thy will be done, on earth as it is in heaven."

Personal Application Questions

1. Think of several examples of how you experience the "already-not-yet-ness" of the kingdom of God in your life.

2. Do you find yourself wanting to enjoy the gift of the kingdom of God without being subject to the demands of the kingdom of God? In what specific ways do you struggle with this?

3. Have you ever been caught in a theological tug-of-war over the concept of healing? How does an understanding of the kingdom of God help you in this area?

4. How have you personally experienced the King's restoration through healing, help, and hope?

5. How could you be an agent of restoration, bringing the King's healing, help, or hope into the life of another person this week?

PART 2

About the Families

6

On Coming to Terms with a New Reality

Mercy is a voluntary sorrow which enjoins itself to the suffering of another. —St. Gregory of Nyssa

What a difference a day makes. There are some events in life that seem to change the world forever. I will always remember what I was doing on that unforgettable day. Freddy's best friend, Douglas, had just returned home from Children's Hospital of Philadelphia where he had successfully undergone a high-risk surgical procedure on his neck. Hoping to provide his mother with a few extra hours of sleep after an exhausting week in the hospital, I arrived at their home around 8:30 in the morning. Thirteen-year-old Douglas was already awake and dressed, adjusting admirably to the contraption of rods, screws, and bolts that stabilized his head and neck. We sat down together and began to talk as he flipped through the TV channels, searching for something interesting to watch. Not being much of a television viewer, I wasn't paying close attention to what was on the screen. As we were chatting, Douglas began to get frustrated while operating the remote control. "The same thing's on *every* channel!" he said in an exasperated tone of voice. I looked at the screen and saw varying images of billowing smoke pouring from a skyscraper as the channels flipped by. "Douglas, this looks important. Maybe we'd better stop and see what it is."

As the second plane plowed into the south tower of the World Trade Center on live camera, my mind seemed frozen in time as I tried to fathom what was happening. Shocked by the events that unfolded before us, each unbelievable image was replaced by an increasingly horrific one. First the attacks on the north tower, south tower, and Pentagon came in almost methodical sequence. In between came the heart-wrenching glimpses of people leaning out of and jumping from the smoke-engulfed floors of the World Trade Centers. Aware that the buildings were still full of thousands of people, the agonizingly unthinkable took place as the south tower collapsed upon itself in a thunderous roar. Next, as the realization arrived that more attacks were still in operation a news flash reported the downing of Flight 93 in our own state of Pennsylvania. Finally, crushing all hope, the north tower succumbed to the inability of its beams to withstand the searing heat of the fire caused by the jet fuel. With apprehension Douglas turned to me and asked, *"When will it stop?"* And then, *"Are we safe?"*

September 11 brought about unwelcome changes that have forever impacted how we see our world, how we live, and how we perceive our future. Terrorism came to our shores in a magnitude that we could not ignore. It was as if scales fell from our eyes, and we were able to see the dramatic effects of the fall in bold relief—raw things from which we had been able to insulate ourselves in "civilized" modern life: senseless pain, torturous suffering, intentional evil, and the white-hot fury of open hatred. While we had come to expect terrorist activity in other parts of the world, we were unaccustomed to its violence within our borders. Now we had to grapple with terrorism in our midst and all of the life-changing implications of that. Accepting this new reality continues to alter many dimensions of American life and touches the lives of others around the globe.

When disability strikes a family, it is akin to a September 11 experience. It is shocking. The mind and soul grapple to fathom what is happening. Nothing is ever the same again. How the family sees the world, how they live, and how they perceive their future are forever altered. Even if their world-view of disability allows them to comprehend it as a "normal part of life in an abnormal world," that doesn't mean they ever expected disability to knock on *their* door. For most of us, disability is only a normal part of life if it is in *somebody else's world*. The presence of disability causes families to come face-to-face with some of the harsh realities of the fall that they might have successfully evaded before. The initial experience of hearing the pronouncement is raw and painful. "Mental retardation." "Irreversible paralysis." "Brain damage." "Permanent loss of vision." "Dementia." "Mental Illness." The list goes on and on. Who is ever truly prepared to hear such descriptors about the condition of their child, spouse, parent, or sibling?

In addition to the diagnosis and all of its long-term implications, the life of a family is often turned upside down by the onslaught of a series of immediate medical and therapeutic interventions. It is not uncommon for the medical component to be crisis oriented. For example, the car crash that caused paralysis has left the individual in immediate need of multiple, complicated surgeries. Perhaps the baby born with Down syndrome has a heart condition so severe that waiting more than a few days to intervene will threaten his young life. Unless a shunt is inserted without delay to drain the fluid from her brain, the newborn with spina bifida might suffer irreversible consequences. A feeding tube. A respirator. A blood transfusion. Similar questions are uttered, *"When will it stop?"* and *"Are we safe?"*

In the aftermath of the events of September 11, who was affected by that experience? Was it limited to the approximately three thousand individuals who lost their lives that day and their immediate families and friends, or did it extend further? Immediately, we recognize that the impact was national in scope, in fact, international. In a corresponding way, disability doesn't just happen to an individual; it affects the entire extended family. Disability is a family affair. It touches parents, spouses, grandparents, siblings, and in-laws. The same holds true for the church: the family of believers is involved—whether it recognizes it or not—and forever changed by the new reality of disability.

How can the church develop a compassionate response to the family that is coming to terms with the new reality of disability in its life? What is needed in these earliest of stages, so that the family experiences the "healing hands of the King" through the hands of his church? St. Gregory of Nyssa once defined mercy as "a voluntary sorrow which enjoins itself to the suffering of another." To enjoin itself effectively to the struggles of a family that is just beginning to navigate the waters of disability, the community of believers needs to understand what the family is *experiencing* and learn to identify what the family *needs* so that the church may respond to those needs in meaningful ways.

Understanding What a Family Is Experiencing

When a family first encounters the reality of disability, it will experience a myriad of changes and will not likely be afforded the luxury of dealing with them in an orderly fashion. Adjustments must be attempted simultaneously on multiple frontiers. A family may find itself tested in ways and degrees that it has never before encountered.

Grief

The first and most intense experience of the family is one of grief. Grief is a natural response to loss. Disability can represent many types of loss. For someone who has become disabled later in life or who encounters a degenerative disability, it can represent the *loss of capacity* and all the accompanying frustrations that exist when previously easy-to-accomplish tasks become increasingly difficult, perhaps impossible. Parents whose child has been diagnosed with a disability experience the sense of a *loss of expectations*—and the associated grief that comes with having a child who is markedly different from the one whom they had anticipated. This does not imply that the parents won't love the child who *has* entered their lives. Indeed, they may eventually find their capacity to love expanded beyond their wildest expectations. However, there will be a significant grief that needs to be experienced even as they attempt to fully embrace the child who has arrived. Over the years, this sense of loss will often be revisited when typical milestones in a child's life are encountered under altered circumstances for *this* child. These milestones may include birthdays, graduations, going off to college, and other rites of passage.

When a personality-altering disability occurs, such as a dementia, a family will likely grieve over the *loss of the "person" whom they once knew*, but who is rapidly slipping relationally from their grasp. Other forms of loss exist in the *crushing of hopes and dreams* or the *wrenching of a perception of control over one's life*. Families need the opportunity to work through the stages of healthy grief, which may include periods of denial, isolation, anger, bargaining, depression, and acceptance.[1]

Family Adjustments

Since families consist of a set of interdependent relationships, the whole system must adapt when an individual within it becomes disabled. The changes required will depend on whether the individual with the disability is a child or an adult in the household, and will depend on the nature of the disability itself. These types of adjustments can be extremely stressful on a family, especially as the family members are simultaneously attempting to address their own grief issues along with an abundance of other concerns. At the same time, "real life" marches on—children require care, meals need to be cooked, laundry must be washed, and bills pile up waiting to be paid. Everyday living can become overwhelming. Consciously or unconsciously, the family will expend precious amounts of energy seeking to find and establish a "new normal" life.

Medical Issues

Virtually all disabling conditions require some type of medical involvement that will have an impact on the family. The intensity of medical intervention will differ depending on the particular situation. In any case, the family will often be dealing with a host of new medical professionals, trying to comprehend the diagnosis, and struggling to become educated in the nature of the disabling condition and all of its implications. In addition, sometimes complex ethical issues exist with pursuing or choosing to not pursue different treatment options, and many families are not prepared to be thrust unexpectedly into this realm.

On a more practical level, the amount of medical paperwork is likely to increase dramatically. This can result in time-consuming encounters with insurance companies and medical providers to maintain accurate records and ensure timely payment of expenses. Keeping track of the flow of diagnostic information and constantly changing treatment plans can be a daunting task.

Financial Issues

Financial strain can occur as a result of the increased demand for medical and therapeutic services. What if the family does not have medical insurance, or what if insurance does not cover many of their medical expenses? What happens when the primary wage earner becomes disabled? What about the loss of income that occurs when the onset of disability requires that an employed adult now be physically available at all times to care for another family member who is disabled? There are many other hidden costs associated with disability. At times, structural modifications need to be made to an existing home to accommodate life with the newly disabled individual. In other situations, the family will need to purchase costly alternatives for transportation, such as a van that is wheelchair-accessible. The nonmedical expenses of hospitalization can be surprisingly costly. These can include parking fees, cafeteria meals, and hotel expenses for family members.

Financial pressures can drive families to take drastic measures. I know. In retrospect I can't believe I had the mental agility to respond in the way I did while in a state of exhaustion. When Timmy was twelve weeks old, I took him to the hospital for a routine cardiology checkup. Immediately after the checkup, he was admitted to the intermediate care unit with a raging case of bacterial spinal meningitis. His life was in the balance for the first week, until his condition stabilized. I stayed on the hospital grounds for seven days, until a friend gently urged me to go home and sleep. Confident that the worst of Timmy's experience was behind him, I headed to the parking lot on the evening of the seventh day to drive home.

In the chaos of Timmy's emergency admission the week before, I had failed to get my parking ticket validated by the cardiology clinic. When I reached the hospital parking lot gate, the attendant replied, "That will be thirty-seven dollars." "*What*? I don't have thirty-seven dollars! I expected to be here for only an hour or two," I sputtered, attempting to relay my story to the attendant. She was belligerent. There were rules. Still in a state of shock that the attendant was so unmoved by my predicament—and highly motivated to go home at last—I noticed a sign behind her head. It stated: *Lost Tickets—$5.00.* Appealing to her rules-oriented demeanor, I cocked my head and tried again, "Excuse me, but does that sign mean that the exit fee for *any* lost ticket is five dollars?"

"Why, yes, it does," she dutifully responded. With that, I tossed my ticket over my shoulder into the back seat, grinned at her, and pleaded, "Oops. I guess I lost my ticket. *Please* let me go home!" Exasperated, she raised the parking gate after lecturing me not to do it again. I assured her that I had no intention of repeating the experience and gladly handed her the five dollars. A story about thirty-seven dollars is funny. The reality of bills totaling $37,000 or $370,000 is no laughing matter. Yet that is exactly the predicament that many families encounter.

Concerns for the Future

If we are honest with ourselves, every Christian struggles with the tension between planning for the future and faith. There is a healthy tension between being a good steward of the resources God has provided and trusting him to supply what we need. An equilibrium also exists between pursuing dreams or goals for our future and accepting God's perfect will—the events of which might never have been in *our* version of the plan—but have always been in *his*. Disability brings with it an entire revaluating of a family's perceptions about the future. Part of the grief process is realigning expectations about the future. When a spouse is diagnosed with dementia at age fifty-five, it radically changes that couple's plans for retirement. If a baby is born with a significantly disabling condition, many questions arise for his parents about who will care for him when they are gone.

Attempting to extrapolate life into the future and to grapple with those probable differences is a very real part of the struggle for those newly impacted by disability—a challenge that never entirely goes away. It also always, eventually, leads back to the same reality that we all face. God alone knows what the future holds, and he will ultimately supply our needs in it. Every family facing disability for the first time will find themselves, at times, functioning like a yo-yo—anxiously extrapolating out to the future—and then snapping back to the challenges of the present. Jesus' words that follow his reminders of our heavenly Father's care can ease the family's tension: "Therefore do not worry about tomorrow, for tomorrow will worry about itself. Each day has enough trouble of its own" (Matt. 6:34).

Legal Issues

Closely tied to concerns for the future are legal issues. When a family addresses disability in their midst, the disability often has legal ramifications as well, particularly if the individual has a cognitive or intellectual disability. This may impact all of a family's legal documentation, including financial accounts, wills, and medical directives. All of these matters must be explored and addressed with an attorney experienced in disability law. The significance of these legal matters may be very weighty and at times urgent. Their resolution, however, requires time, energy, and focus that the family may not possess.

Social Issues

While coming to terms with disability, family members may confront social issues. Responsibility for educating extended family and friends about the nature of the specific disability usually falls on their shoulders even as they are trying to process their own feelings about the disability. Encounters with prejudice, stereotypes, and just a general awkwardness with the subject of disability may make previously welcomed social situations extremely difficult. The family may experience the extremes of alienation from friends, or boundary-violating intrusions by well-meaning but misguided people.

Testing of Their Faith

We all face times throughout our lives when our faith is severely tested. A personal encounter with disability can be one of those times. Family members may face a vast array of legitimate spiritual struggles challenging them to wrestle with biblical truths about God's love, his goodness, and his sovereignty over all things. They may also realize a need to exercise a deeper dependence on God to provide for them in their circumstances. This can be a very vulnerable time but also a significant time of spiritual growth in the life of a family.

Identifying and Responding to What a Family Needs

Understanding what a family is *experiencing* is a necessary condition to showing compassion. Extending mercy is impossible if we don't comprehend the nature of another's struggle. At the same time, identifying what the family *needs* and responding to those needs are the steps that will make mercy a reality.

Privacy to Process

To "enjoin" together with those who are grief-stricken means to experience a dimension of their grief with them. While it is possible for families or individuals to become "stuck" in their grief process, people are more often guilty of rushing others through bereavement, rather than giving them permission to take the time they need to mourn and come to a sense of resolution. The demands of the grief process and the potentially overwhelming circumstances facing a family touched by disability require time and privacy to process. It is unreasonable to expect family members to always be able or willing to articulate their feelings and concerns. Quite possibly, they may not even understand them yet! Consider the writings of David in the Psalms. Many of his words included in the Scriptures depict the anguish of a heart that is privately wrestling with his circumstances and seeking to understand God's role in them.

My God, my God, why have you forsaken me?
  Why are you so far from saving me,
  so far from the words of my groaning?
O my God, I cry out by day, but you do not answer,
  by night, and am not silent. (Ps. 22:1–2)

Turn to me and be gracious to me,
  for I am lonely and afflicted.
The troubles of my heart have multiplied;
  free me from my anguish. (Ps. 25:16–17)

To you I call, O LORD my Rock;
  do not turn a deaf ear to me.
For if you remain silent,
  I will be like those who have gone down to the pit.
Hear my cry for mercy
  as I call to you for help,
as I lift my hands
  toward your Most Holy Place. (Ps. 28:1–2)

The recording of his words both legitimizes the struggle and permits us a glimpse into this painful, private process.

Presence

However, the right to privacy is not a call for abandonment! The family needs to know the loving and supportive presence of others now more than ever. Family members will need to be reassured that their friends and extended family are committed to them for the long haul. When Timmy was born, God's presence became very real to us, in part, through the loving, caring involvement of our family and our church. Our extended family members live in other states, so visits from them were particularly cherished. My brother and his family came to our home to meet Timmy when he was one week old. We spent a wonderful afternoon talking and laughing and playing with Freddy and their children. When our time grew to a close and the sun began to set, I still remember standing at the upstairs window watching pensively as my brother's car backed out of the driveway. From behind the glass, I began to cry out to him with surprising and uncontrollable sobs, "Don't *leave* me here!" There was just something incredibly reassuring about the presence of my older sibling who was not just my blood relative, but also my brother in Christ. He was the hands and feet of Jesus to me that day, and it was so difficult to see him go.

Families also need people who are good listeners. While this is true all along the path, it is an essential aspect of presence in the early stages. In the biblical account of Job, one of the things that Job's friends did well was to sit with him for seven days without saying a word—sharing his grief through presence. Not passing judgment on the feelings of others, but giving them the opportunity to process their emotions is an essential part of being a good listener. People who are in the midst of deep grief and struggle do not need "easy" answers. They require caring people who—through works more than words—lovingly point them back, over and over again, to "the One who is the Answer."[2]

In addition, families need people who are willing to roll up their sleeves and help. When Timmy was frequently hospitalized as an infant, dozens of meals were delivered, teams of people cleaned our house, individuals sent us money for the increased expenses we were facing, and friends and family provided child care for Freddy for weeks at a time. We also had so many visitors in the hospital that the nursing staff frequently noted the volume of love and support we received. When Timmy was at home, two high school girls from church watched the boys at our house every Sunday morning so we could attend church, as Timmy's fragile health at that time didn't permit him to be in large public gatherings. Another friend took Freddy to gymnastics every week while I attended early intervention classes with Timmy so he could receive a variety of therapies. My parents funded "Mother's Day Out" so that I had one quiet morning a week when Freddy was out, and he had the opportunity to have fun with other children. Many creative, helpful, and practical deeds of mercy were extended to us during those early months of adjustment.

Normalcy

The disruptive nature of disability varies from situation to situation. But in every case, it requires some adjustment from "life as it was" to "life as it is" or possibly preparing for "life as it will be." Establishing a "new equilibrium" or "new normal" is a time-consuming process that requires patience. Wherever normal patterns or routines can be maintained, especially when young children are involved, the greater the sense of normalcy the family will experience. It is essential that family members preserve a sense of dignity and appropriate control over their own lives. It is respectful to ask the individuals in the family what they want and need. Don't presume anything. If they don't seem to know what they desire or require, then there is the freedom to offer to help them evaluate their needs.

When assistance is offered, the boundaries of the family need to be respected. A "no" must be honored for what it is. Remember, "love is patient, love is kind. . . . It is not self-seeking" (1 Cor. 13:4–5). In attempting to minister to others, we have to be sure we know whom we are trying to help. Be careful if the desire to assist is rooted in the need to "do something" in order to allay a personal sense of helplessness.

On a very specific note, consider the normal response when a typical baby is born to a family. Usually, it is a time of tremendous joy and heartfelt celebration. In his epistle to the Romans, the apostle Paul reminds us to "Rejoice with those who rejoice; mourn with those who mourn" (Rom. 12:15). Just as Paul communicates those two separate mandates in the same sentence, so must the church come alongside a family whose newborn is diagnosed with a disability and participate in both realities. The first reality is that the family and the church have received the priceless gift of a new life—a life endowed with the image of God himself and full of unique potential. The life of *every* new baby is cause for celebration and congratulations. Yet too many families have been robbed of this normal joy when others fail to recognize this, seeing only the disability of the infant.

At the same time, the birth of such a precious covenant child has ushered in some harsh realities and a sense of deep grief. Just because disability is a normal part of life in an abnormal world does not mean it is *easy*. Christ was always willing to engage people in their pain, and we must be too. Reading through the gospels and observing Jesus' interactions with people, it is evident that his primary concern was always for the individual before him, not for himself or his own reputation. Jesus demonstrated for us how to mourn with those who mourn. He also showed us how to rejoice with those who rejoice. It is incredibly challenging to learn how to do *both simultaneously*, but it is so important to the family of a newborn with a disability. When Timmy was several weeks old, a friend from church came by to visit. As she sat in our living room cradling Timmy, she looked at me and said, "You know, he's really cute . . . anyway." Ouch. Granted, it would have been easier to hear, "My, he's a beautiful baby. How hard it must be for you to process some of the challenges that this precious little boy will likely face in life." But in retrospect, I really admire this woman's genuine attempt to recognize the wonderful gift that Timmy was, and to acknowledge the difficulties she anticipated would be ours. Rejoice with those who rejoice; mourn with those who mourn.

Summary

What a difference a day makes. When that day occurs in the life of a family at your church—and it will—please *be there*. Be there to understand what they are experiencing. Be

94

there to help them identify their needs. Be there to respond to those needs as the practical presence of Jesus in their lives. For the family that is coming to terms with the new reality of disability, it will make all the difference.

Personal Application Questions

1. Do you know someone who has encountered a "September 11 experience" with disability? How did their friends and family respond?

2. Have you ever considered that disability is a family affair both for the biological family and for the covenant family of God? How does this change the way that you respond to the parents, spouses, children, siblings, and grandparents of those who are disabled?

3. Of all the changes a family is experiencing with the onset of disability, which ones are the easiest for you to understand? Which ones are the most difficult?

4. How do you strike a delicate balance between "privacy to process" and "presence"? Do you think the balance is the same for every family? Why or why not?

5. What are three practical things that you could do to promote normalcy for a family with young children when that family encounters the onset of disability?

7

On Negotiating a Path to Acceptance

Peace is the deliberate adjustment of my life to the will of God.
—Anonymous

For generations, my husband's family has made an annual pilgrimage. The long journey embarked upon every summer is steeped with familiarity, tradition, and ritual. No less significant than a sojourner's passage to Mecca is the Hubach family's annual expedition to Maine. It is a journey that every Fred Hubach must make, not just once in his lifetime, but preferably as often as possible. Frederick George Hubach took his son, Frederick Willis Hubach, who in turn took his son, Frederick Robert Hubach, who predictably takes his son, Frederick Wesley Hubach. Frederick Wesley is my son Freddy. And I believe that Freddy is, perhaps, as intoxicated with Maine as all of the previous Freds combined.

Whether it is the fresh air, the clear water, the joy of the combined attention of his parents and grandparents, the eerie sounds of the loons upon the lake at night, the crackle of the fire on a cool morning, the heavy scent of pine mingled with the sweet smell of grasses and ferns, or the sheer thrill of summer freedom as expressed in a full-throttle boat ride—Freddy has "the fever." Of course, fishing is an essential part of the Maine experience as well. Generations of Freds have fish stories to tell. Tales of fish that were caught, fish that were *almost* caught, and of course the ones that got away. But my favorite fish story is about Freddy and the fish that never even showed up.

If there ever was a perfect Maine day, it was like this: hot sun, cool air, and a crystal-blue sky. And like any Maine day, regardless of the weather, it was a perfect day for fishing. Lots of fishing. Hours and hours of fishing. Freddy was seven years old, and he had yet to discover that, apparently, the joy of fishing is found not in just actually catching them, but in simply waiting for them. This is a reality about fishing that, personally, I have yet to appreciate fully. After sweltering in the sun for what seemed like an eternity without even a nibble, Freddy finally became exasperated. He turned desperately and looked around the boat, inhabited by his father and grandfather, and stammered, *"We're experiencing a bad hand of Providence!"*

How do *you* respond to difficulty in life? What happens when your expectations don't correspond to your reality? Do you still see the goodness of God, or do you feel like you've been dealt "a bad hand of Providence"? In his book titled *The Road Less Traveled*, M. Scott Peck makes the following observations:

> Life is difficult.
> This is a great truth, one of the greatest truths. It is a great truth because once we truly see this truth, we transcend it. Once we truly know that life is difficult—once we truly understand and accept it—then life is no longer difficult. Because once it is accepted, the fact that life is difficult no longer matters.[1]

Whatever one thinks of Peck's psychology or his theology, he has hit the bull's-eye in identifying a decisive struggle of the human heart. It is true: we do not want to accept that life is difficult. Relationships are problematic, circumstances can be incredibly tough, and losses can be staggeringly painful. Even fishing can be challenging! Because of the fall, a level of difficulty permeates all of creation—and it invades our personal lives as well. Perhaps we struggle to accept that life is difficult because, deep inside, we intuitively understand that life is not as it was intended to be; difficulty is a normal part of life in an *abnormal* world. We long for the restoration of all things even if we cannot articulate the reasons for that heartfelt yearning.

Much of our twenty-first-century American life is organized around denying the reality of life's difficulty. We can surround ourselves with material comforts that give us the false sense of security that, maybe, life is not so difficult after all. We can create an illusion of control that, perhaps, we really are the masters of our own destiny. However, when the reality of disability strikes, neither a thousand trips to Wal-Mart nor unlimited funds in a retirement account can insulate the blow. When disability touches the life of a family, it is the startling splash-of-a-bucket-of-ice-water-in-the-face that reminds us that, indeed, life *is* difficult. And we are *not* in control. Accepting disability and all its ramifications is a challenging task. How is that accomplished? Is it enough to simply acknowledge that "life is difficult," or does it require something more?

A Definition of Acceptance

The family's concept of acceptance is crucial. Accepting disability in its midst is critical to the spiritual, emotional, and relational health of each family member. *Acceptance*, in this context, could be defined as: *developing peace about the presence of disability in the life of a family.* The definition is not static because acceptance is not an event or a place. It is a process. Acceptance is all about embracing reality as it is right now, and the willingness to embrace reality as it will be when the future becomes the present.

Embracing Reality through Conflict

The process of developing peace is at the core of acceptance because nurturing peace implies diminishing strife. But a word of warning is in order: developing peace is not the same as resignation. Resignation is a counterfeit peace. It involves suppressing the conflict, not resolving it. Fostering genuine peace comes only through the hard work of struggle, while the cheap peace of resignation eventually reaps a harvest of bitterness. What are the areas of conflict that require genuine resolution on the part of individuals and family systems in order to negotiate a path to acceptance?

Releasing

A significant dimension of the grieving process over disability has to do with *releasing expectations*. In the many losses associated with disability, loss of expectations can be one of the most powerful ones. Whether we recognize it or not, we all have implicit expectations about the future that reside in our minds. Maybe they are expectations of what our children will be like, what our jobs will be like, or what our retirement years will look like. The onset of disability often, if not always, requires a realignment of those expectations. The accompanying sense of loss is quite genuine, and the waters of grief can be deep.

During late springtime, before Timmy was born, Fred and Freddy and I visited friends in Myrtle Beach, South Carolina. Much of our time was spent playing on the sand and in the surf. Our family has marvelous memories of time together with precious friends. One of the photos from that trip eventually ended up on my parents' refrigerator. It was a snapshot of Freddy, my friend Karen, and me at the seaside. At the time the picture was taken, I was about six weeks pregnant. So, actually, it was a picture of Freddy, Karen, me—and Timmy, *incognito*. Several months after Timmy was born, while still working through the initial stages of grief, I found myself in my parents' kitchen gazing at the refrigerator. As I stared at the photo in its magnetic frame, it struck me like a thunderbolt. *The only thing that changed when Timmy was born was my set of expectations.* Even at the time the shutter was released on the camera that day, Timmy already had Down syndrome. And he had since his conception. Nothing about reality had ever changed—just my expectations. I'm not entirely sure why that thought was immediately comforting, but it was. Perhaps it was because I realized afresh what I already knew—that God was not surprised by these events, only I was. And that the "something wrong" that needed to change had to do with my own perceptions, not with Timmy himself. The earliest aspects of developing peace about disability require us to begin the challenging, painful work of releasing our expectations.

Redirecting

When an earthquake strikes, it occurs without warning, and its effects are usually far-reaching. In the aftermath of an earthquake, the entire community must assess what has happened and must develop a plan to redirect their lives. We have all seen pictures of an earthquake-ravaged area and have felt overwhelmed at the obviously daunting task of restructuring lives in its aftermath. The same is true with disability. The degree of devastation varies widely from family to family. The focus of a family facing permanent disability is not to rebuild life as it was, but to *redirect by building a new life that incorporates disability into it.* Embracing reality for what it is frees up a family to make all the necessary adjustments for successful living. Denying the reality of what is true and seeking only to regain what was lost is an exercise in futility that leads to increased grief and prolonged frustration.

When Timmy was about six months old, we went on another vacation to the beach. After sitting on the sand for a spell, I sensed the need to get up and stretch my legs. Cradling Timmy in my arms, I strolled down along the edge of the water. Eventually, we came upon an amusing sight. About ten older ladies were individually perched upon an equal number of neatly aligned beach chairs. Their seats were adjacent to where the surf methodically rolled in and just as predictably receded until the next wave arrived. Immediately in front of the row of chairs was a small wall of sand that had been constructed, presumably, to allow the ladies in the chairs to keep their feet dry. The sand, however, was insufficient for the task of holding back the incoming tide. As each new wave tore apart a piece of the barricade, several of the ladies frantically ran back and forth attempting to rebuild the fortification before the foaming surf struck again. It was obvious to the casual observer that these women needed a reality adjustment. It was time to stop rebuilding the wall. It was time to start moving the chairs.

Upon reflection it occurred to me that this was a glimpse, at least in part, of my life with Timmy. In some ways I had accepted the reality of his diagnosis, and yet in other ways I was unwilling to "move my chair." Instead, I kept rebuilding the walls around our lives in an increasingly obvious exercise in futility. Through that visual image, it struck me that perhaps I was approaching his therapies as ways to *attempt to change him*, instead of ways to *enable him to achieve his highest potential*. My walk on the beach that day was a turning point in my relationship with Timmy, because accepting the reality of disability is also about accepting the person who is disabled. It is about receiving them for who they are, not who we wish they would be. Acceptance requires redirecting our lives to a place that fully enfolds them into it, with all of the needs they might bring and all of the blessings they offer.

Responsibility

A third aspect of embracing reality through conflict comes in the form of *incorporating new responsibilities*. From time to time, I have had my moments of what I call "emotional foot-stomping." You know what I mean—those moments when everything in your inner being screams, "I DON'T WANT TO *DO* THIS!" When Timmy was just a few months old, I specifically remember having one of those moments. It might have been one of the first, but it certainly was not the last. Honestly, I don't remember the events of the day and why such a feeling of being overwhelmed washed over me at that particular time. All I recall is the sense of being besieged with massive emotions of resistance and defiance. Truth be known, I did not want to work this hard. This was not what I had bargained for. Never in my wildest dreams had I envisioned such a broad spectrum of needs all packed into one child—*who was my responsibility.* I felt trapped, and I didn't like it one bit.

Just as I was actually beginning to relish being in my pity party, I looked down at Timmy who was lying on my lap with his head at my knees and his feet against my waist. His eyes gazed straight into mine and it was as if my heart could clearly hear him say, "Won't you help me, Mommy?" My stubborn selfishness dissolved and, releasing a flood of tears, I blurted out to him, "Of course I will!"

New responsibilities are part and parcel of the package of disability. For caregivers, the load of new responsibilities can seem utterly staggering. Coming in virtually an infinite variety of tasks, they can include acquiring and executing different therapies: physical, occupational, speech, vision, and cognitive (to name a few). Medical appointments. Intensive medical care. Equipment acquisition. Practicing feeding techniques. Laboring for additional finances. Implementing behavior plans. Meeting with social workers, therapists, teachers, physicians, psychiatrists, and on and on. If the primary wage earner becomes disabled, sometimes the spouse needs to seek and obtain employment while juggling the responsibilities of care. For an adult individual who becomes disabled, there are many new duties associated with personal rehabilitation. And siblings feel the changes too. By necessity, carefree childhoods are transformed overnight as children attempt to adapt to all the changes swirling around them and to the new responsibilities to their disabled family member that inevitably come their way.

How does a family find peace in the midst of all these new responsibilities? The best answer that I have heard is found in the profound little volume entitled *The Power of the Powerless*. Within those pages, Christopher de Vinck beautifully articulates the life lessons he learned through his brother Oliver:

> I grew up in the house where my brother was on his back in his bed for thirty-two years, in the same corner of his room, under the same window, beside the same yellow walls. He was blind, mute. His legs were twisted. He didn't have the strength to lift his head or the intelligence to learn anything.[2]

Reflecting on his parents' perspective on their responsibilities to Oliver, de Vinck recalls the following:

> I asked my father, "How did you care for Oliver for thirty-two years?" "It was not thirty-two years," he said. "I just asked myself, 'Can I feed Oliver today?' and the answer was always, 'Yes, I can.'" We lived with Oliver moment by moment.[3]

Living with disability doesn't require having the strength for tomorrow today. Finding peace in the midst of the responsibilities that accompany disability means learning, in God's strength, to live moment by moment.

Relinquishing

Control is an illusion, but it is an illusion that most of us enjoy at one level or another. As Christians we may dutifully confess that "God is in control," but our behavior often belies that statement. When calamity enters the life of a family, the façade comes crashing down, and we are left exposed. At the risk of stating the obvious: no one goes out seeking to acquire a disability. It is something that happens to an individual and consequently impacts the entire family. Any illusions of personal control over one's circumstances are shattered by the entry of disability into the scenery of family life. Suddenly the previously unspoken question stares us boldly in the face, "Who's really in charge here?"

Responding to that question is akin to standing at a fork in the road—one that may be revisited at times in the journey toward acceptance. Adopting the right choice makes all the difference. Countless manuscripts have been written on the topic of God's role in suffering, or the lack thereof. The intent of this book is not to explore the depths of that question. Instead, I would propose to you that the possible responses are simple, like the fork in the road. Either God is sovereign *and* good, or he is not. I have a friend who once told me, "All relationships are like bridges. They are built on the two trusses of trust and respect." The same principles can be applied to our relationship with God in the context of suffering. If God is not powerful, he cannot be trusted to "come through" for us. If he is not good, he is not worthy of our respect. Either God is both sovereign *and* good, or he is not.

During the first months of Timmy's life I experienced an intense struggle with relinquishing illusions of control over my life that I hadn't even realized existed to such an extent. With each heartrending, life-threatening event in Timmy's path, it was as if God was gently prying my white-knuckled fingers off the steering wheel of my life until I had nothing to hold onto—except for God himself. At the time, the analogy I shared with my pastor was that my life was like a bursting dike with at least eleven holes in it and I only had ten fingers. There were days I remember hunching over the kitchen sink begging for God to give me the strength to get through the next ten minutes. Just the next ten minutes.

As 1992 drew to a close and the Thanksgiving holiday approached, Timmy (almost eleven months old) had successfully survived his heart surgery and all of the illnesses that had plagued him in his previously weakened condition. Reflecting back on the events of the year, I realized that there were many things for which I could give thanks. But when I spoke up at the Thanksgiving Eve service at our church, what I said went something like this: "What I am most thankful for this year is simply this. That God is who he says he is, and that he will do what he says he will do. Even when my heart was broken into a million tiny pieces, and I didn't know for sure what else was true anymore, I could hold onto this: That God is who he says he is, and he will do what he says he will do."

And that is enough. God releases his power when we relinquish ours. In that truth great freedom is found. For when we recognize that God is in charge, we don't have to try to be. Surely we have individual responsibilities, and that is an important part of embracing reality, but we are not ultimately responsible for *outcomes*—God is.

Relinquishing control to God, who is great and good, is at the heart of the following verses written by seventeenth-century hymn writer Samuel Rodigast:

> Whate'er my God ordains is right: his holy will abideth;
> I will be still whate'er he doth, and follow where he
>   guideth.
> He is my God; though dark my road, he holds me that I
>   shall not fall:
> Wherefore to him I leave it all.
>
> Whate'er my God ordains is right: he never will deceive
>   me;
> He leads me by the proper path; I know he will not leave
>   me.
> I take, content, what he hath sent; his hand can turn my
>   griefs away,
> And patiently I wait his day.

Whate'er my God ordains is right: though now this cup, in
    drinking,
May bitter seem to my faint heart, I take it, all unshrink-
    ing.
My God is true; each morn anew sweet comfort yet shall
    fill my heart,
And pain and sorrow shall depart.

Whate'er my God ordains is right: here shall my stand be
    taken;
Though sorrow, need, or death be mine, yet am I not for-
    saken.
My Father's care is round me there; he holds me that I
    shall not fall:
And so to him I leave it all.[4]

This is the reality of biblical faith—that life is hard, *and* God is good—and that God has both the power and the desire to work all things together for the good of those who love him (Rom. 8:28). A developing peace finds its deepest roots in relinquishing control and abandoning ourselves to genuine faith in our heavenly Father, who is worthy of our trust and respect.

Realizing

The beauty of embracing reality is that even though life is difficult, reality is not all negative. True, it requires releasing our expectations, redirecting our lives, exercising new responsibilities, and relinquishing control. The pathway to acceptance, however, also involves *realizing the benefits* of the place where God has taken us. Making our peace with diffi-culty frees us to find the beauty in the ashes too. When we stop focusing on the difficulty and start focusing on God's good-ness, we discover manifestations of it in many places.

On the day after Timmy was born, my parents made the journey to the hospital to meet him and be with us. Being early January, there was a fresh dusting of snow on the

Maryland farmland as they drove along the highway. The flakes of snow sparkled like millions of tiny diamonds on the hard earth. "Look how beautiful that is!" my mother expressed. As the dazzling snow captured her attention, she mused, "Timmy will teach us to see the world as we have never been able to see it before." And he truly has.

The Role of the Church

The Bible tells us to "seek peace and pursue it" (Ps. 34:14b). This is precisely what a family is attempting to do when it is striving to accept disability and all its ramifications. Exactly what do families who are negotiating the path toward acceptance need from the church?

Patience and Permission for the Process

Sometimes, one of the greatest barriers to patience with others in the process toward acceptance has much more to do with our own discomfort than with a genuine concern for the family. We are uncomfortable with the erratic nature of the journey. The raw emotions and direct questions make us squirm. Having not experienced life at this depth of struggle, perhaps we're not sure that we really want to. Or maybe we're frightened that in our ignorance, we'll make it all worse rather than better. But God can use us in spite of ourselves when we are willing to risk demonstrating his love and patience to others.

In the days prior to having children, my husband and I made a rather dramatic move to Pennsylvania from the hustle and bustle of years in Washington, D.C. Eager to escape the financial and cultural pressures of the Washingtonian lifestyle, we bought our first house and settled into a sleepy little town in central Pennsylvania. While there were many benefits to this move, it was a challenging adjustment for me personally, as I left a fantastic, upwardly mobile job with an outstanding firm. The type of work that I had done in the D.C.

area was not readily available in our new location. For months, I searched for new employment to no avail. In addition, I found myself missing my old friends.

In an admittedly self-interested way, I finally decided that perhaps the best way to *get* a friend was to *be* a friend, so I sought out relationships in the women's Bible study at my church. About the same time, one of the women in that group had given birth to a child with multiple, significant medical problems. Looking for a connection, I offered to assist her in whatever ways would be helpful, and as a result I ended up accompanying her to some of their many medical appointments each week. During those rides back and forth to the children's hospital in the next county, Patty and I forged the beginnings of a close friendship. My ignorance about child-rearing in general, and disabling medical conditions in particular, actually made me a well-suited companion. I hadn't a clue how to advise or counsel her, so I mostly just listened as she processed her feelings about the myriad of new responsibilities that their family faced. Having encountered very little real difficulty in my own life, I was not appalled by her struggles, but admired the unedited honesty and courage with which she confronted complex issues about life, death, suffering, and faith.

Three years later, when Timmy was born, guess who was the first person to visit me? It was Patty. When it was my turn to negotiate a path to acceptance, I had the unusual privilege of a seasoned traveler to walk alongside. What an unexpected blessing from my meager efforts at trying to be a good listener. In the end, I was given a gift that far outweighed anything I had invested.

Treating a family with patience and granting permission for the processing of acceptance is an incredible privilege and one that should be entered into with gentle care but without great apprehension. Please don't feel that it is your job to rescue a family from their struggles. It is important for them to learn to come to own them. One of the greatest gifts you can give to a family grappling with disability is the willingness to listen patiently to them share their grief, fears, and concerns. God is not afraid of their hard questions, and you don't need to be either.

Remember: *rushed resolution results in resignation.* And resignation is a counterfeit peace. Help them find the pathway to peace by giving them permission to work through the conflicts that are part of acceptance.

Modeling the Life of Jesus: Full of Grace and Truth

Let's be honest. People who are wrestling with challenging issues can be difficult to be around! Negotiating a path to acceptance is hard work for everyone involved—both those inside and alongside the process. It takes grace, time and again, to respond with compassion to another's suffering time and again. Operating from a posture of grace means recalling that we all share common experiences of brokenness, even if the details are different. Remember: It is *same lake, different boat.*

Walking next to a family engaging the reality of permanent disability also requires being truthful. Grappling honestly with weaknesses in areas of faith, owning the ugliness of harbored prejudices, and grieving the disappointment of shattered dreams is extremely challenging. Families need "truth-tellers" who will lovingly help them face difficult personal issues honestly in the light of biblical truth.

Unfortunately, stories abound of individuals who have seen the struggles of another as a great opportunity to offer a spiritually abusive "Bible-beating."

> *"What sin is there in your life that brought this judgment upon you?"*

> *"If you weren't so stubborn, God wouldn't have had to hit you with a brick to get you to pay attention."*

"If you hadn't been involved in the church split, this wouldn't have happened to your daughter."

All three of these accusations were made toward people I know who were in the process of negotiating a path to acceptance. Can you imagine more hurtful, judgmental words? Loving, gracious truth-tellers don't use the Bible as a wounding weapon; they use it to bring healing balm from the Great Physician himself.

Summary

When someone in your life encounters disability and responds with, "We're experiencing a bad hand of Providence!" will you engage them? Will you walk alongside them in grace and truth as they negotiate a pathway to acceptance? The journey is not for the fainthearted, but the outcome can be beautiful:

> When peace, like a river, attendeth my way,
> When sorrows like sea billows roll;
> Whatever my lot Thou hast taught me to say,
> "It is well, it is well with my soul."[5]

Personal Application Questions

1. Has there been a time in your life when you thought the equivalent of, "We're experiencing a bad hand of Providence!"? What were the circumstances you were experiencing at that time?

2. Why is the pathway to acceptance riddled with conflict? How are those conflicts resolved in order for peace to be fostered?

3. What does the statement "rushed resolution results in resignation" mean?

4. Why can it be so difficult to be around people who are wrestling with challenging issues? How can remembering the concept "same lake, different boat" help you in that difficulty?

5. Why are the qualities of truth and grace inseparable when walking alongside the person who is negotiating a path to acceptance?

8

On Living a New Normal Life

It's all different and it's all the same. —Stephanie Hubach

Ah, childhood. It can be full of captivating moments. Consider, for example, the fascination and sheer excitement of dialing the emergency telephone number 9-1-1—several times in the same week. At first, I rationalized Timmy's growing personal connection with the local 9-1-1 operator as a bad habit that might take a little bit longer to break, since children with Down syndrome tend to learn (and unlearn) things more slowly. Freddy, however, experienced intense mortification every time the operator contacted our house to verify the call. As the frequency of these episodes increased, my sense of exasperation grew as well.

During this aggravating period in our family history, we went on a journey to visit friends for the weekend. The first day we were there, Timmy was swashbuckling his way through their house playing with a *Star Wars* lightsaber. Other than the fact that the flasher in the sword did not operate properly, it was functional for engaging in pretend battles. After Timmy brought the non-operational light beam to my attention, I dismissed him to play, assuring him that the toy was fine the way it was. Then I returned to sipping coffee with our friends.

A few minutes later I heard Timmy calling me from the other room. Finally, I wandered into the location where he thrust the receiver from a Mickey Mouse phone toward me. "It's for you!" he stated emphatically. "For me?" I asked quizzically. "How can that be? This isn't our house!" Insistently, he handed me the phone. As I heard the operator's voice, my heart sank. "Ma'am," she said with that characteristic nasally sound, "we understand that there's an emergency. The young boy told us that someone is choking on a Lifesaver. We've dispatched an ambulance immediately, and they should be there in a few moments." Panicking, I stammered, "No! No! There's no emergency here! P-l-e-a-s-e don't send an ambulance!" Vividly envisioning the scene it would create in the neighborhood cul-de-sac as the ambulance screeched into the driveway with sirens blaring and lights flashing, I began to beg. Confused, the operator replied, "Are you sure? Are you sure there's no one *choking on a Lifesaver?*" "I'm *sure*," I retorted, glaring intently at Timmy over the receiver. As I hung up, staring at him in disbelief, I demanded, "What were you *doing?*" Timidly, and with genuine sincerity, he held up the Star Wars toy. "I have a *broken lightsaber*, so I called 9-1-1 to fix it." Ugh.

Living a "new normal" life with disability is a lot like handling a broken lightsaber. It is about recognizing the difference between the need for crisis intervention and the need for assistance or supports. It involves helping those who surround the family to avoid the extremes of indifference and imposed control. It requires finding the healthy tension point between merciful intervention and familial responsibility; discerning the equilibrium between independence and dependence in a place called "interdependent community."

After the initial shock of disability-related change has been encountered and, even as the path toward acceptance is being negotiated, the family newly touched by disability will be seeking a new state of equilibrium, or a "new normal." Every family can relate to significant changes it has encountered in life and all of the necessary adjustments that are required. Changes can be as common as beginning a new job or purchasing a different house. Or they can involve more stressful issues such as relocating to a new city or the trauma of experiencing a death in the family. Families walk the pathway of familial transformation when a new baby arrives, complete with the blessings and discomfort that come with those adaptations.

The new equilibrium that a family affected by disability seeks is similar to that sought by other families in different types of circumstances. They will work to find their stride as a family, learning to move in step together as a unit—even if they must march to a different drummer from most. As Helen Featherstone states in *A Difference in the Family*, "Differences differ only in degree from those of other families."[1] What *realities* are associated with these differences of degree? What are the *results* of these differences? What *remedies*, if any, are required, and what is the role of the church in that context?

The Realities of the Differences of Degree

Every family faces significant challenges in living and in raising children. But consider the following differences of degree often confronted by families with disabled family members.

Personal Care

Feeding and diapering is an expected duty of normal infant care. As a necessary parental responsibility, it is endurable because there is typically an achievable goal of independence in sight at the end of about two short years. But these responsibilities can carry on for an extended period of time, or even for a lifetime, in families with a disabled family member. Feeding and changing a dependent teenager or an adult family member is quite different from caring for an infant. Toilet training a child with an intellectual disability can be significantly more difficult and time-consuming than teaching a typical toddler. In a different way, personal care for an individual with a spinal cord injury,* for example, can present its own challenges in maintaining a program for bladder and/or bowel management.

Education

Parents want their children to receive a good education. The desire is the same for parents whose children have special needs. Typical children start school at about five years old. Children with developmental disabilities often begin special schooling through early intervention programs as early as five weeks old. However, the difficulties encountered in trying to maneuver the early intervention and special education mazes are immense. Instead of dealing with one teacher, parents must communicate and coordinate with numerous educators, specialists, therapists, and administrators. A working knowledge of special education law is necessary to preserve the programmatic options legally available to one's child.

Parents who desire private Christian schooling for their children almost always find themselves in a dilemma. Often, they encounter statements such as, "Oh, I'm sorry, we can't possibly meet *his* needs. You understand it would be tremendously expensive for us to do *that*." Though the financial impact can be significant in a private educational setting, it would be genuinely encouraging for families to encounter Christian school boards and administrators who are, at a minimum, dedicated to seriously reflecting on their covenantal responsibilities to children with disabilities. An increased commitment to the inclusion of children with disabilities in private Christian schools could provide the motivation to pursue alternative approaches to cost management such as multi-school sharing of special education teachers and resources.

One positive example of a Christian school that endeavors to meet the needs of students with disabilities is Promise

* "Spinal Cord Injury (SCI) is damage to the spinal cord that results in a loss of function such as mobility or feeling. Frequent causes of damage are trauma (car accident, gunshot, falls, etc.) or disease (polio, spina bifida, Friedreich's Ataxia, etc.). The spinal cord does not have to be severed in order for a loss of functioning to occur." (Source: Spinal Cord Injury Resource Center)

Christian Academy in St. Louis, Missouri. Consider the following excerpt from their statement of philosophy:

> Because of the divine mandate for each individual to discover and exercise his or her God given gifts, Promise Christian Academy is charged with enabling students with disabilities to explore and develop those gifts while becoming the people God intends them to be. The school recognizes that God has created all of His children to be mirrors of Himself and equipped them to serve and obey Him. We view children with disabilities as recipients of God's special attention and calling, and our passion is to help all students in the school to realize that God has given them the necessary resources to serve Him and others.[2]

We can hope that Promise Christian Academy is just one of many Christian schools that, in the ensuing years, will catch the vision to meet the needs of students with disabilities in their communities.

Behavior

All parents have the seemingly endless role of teaching their children to behave in appropriate ways as they learn to develop self-control. For some disabilities, behavioral issues are a significant part of daily life. Finding unique and effective ways to teach appropriate behaviors can require tremendous creativity, persistent boundary setting, and immense amounts of emotional energy on the part of caregivers. When the family member has a cognitive disability or a communication disorder, discernment is also necessary. Those engaged with them need to consider whether what is being observed is actually a negative behavior, or is it the result of an attempt at communication on the part of the individual— communication that might be difficult or impossible for them to articulate in any other way. Mounting frustration with failed attempts to communicate can also significantly impact behavior.

At other times intentions are more obvious. One Sunday, when Timmy was eleven, we were having communion in church. He had repeatedly expressed a desire to participate and, rather than dismiss his interest, I attempted to evaluate exactly how much he understood about the sacrament. As the bread was distributed, I reminded him of what it represents. When the cup was passed, I leaned over to him and showed him. Then I queried him and Timmy offered the appropriate response. *This is good . . .* I mused to myself silently, and began to relax into a feeling of satisfaction. But suddenly Timmy leaned over, his eyes staring wildly, and he blurted out in a raspy voice, "It's *poison!* Drink it and go like this!" Whereupon he began grabbing himself around the neck and shaking his head pretending he was choking. While I knew immediately that Timmy was imitating a scene from a Disney movie he had recently viewed, this was not readily apparent to anyone else. As an elder, my husband Fred was in the midst of serving communion, while his family was living out this little drama in our usual location—the front row. Wishing that the earth would open up and swallow me, and momentarily regretting that we had put so much effort into speech therapy, I immediately began to rethink the wisdom of both our location and my timing for this conversation.

As with most families, our family's behavioral challenges have not been limited only to the world of socially appropriate actions, but also to issues of safety, personal boundaries, respect, and countless other dimensions. For some families, though, there are exceedingly difficult dynamics with self-expression and self-injurious behaviors as well. These can be very taxing on family life, sometimes resulting in a level of chaos in which it is difficult to find any sense of normalcy.

Time Management

Twenty-first century American society moves at a dizzying pace. All families struggle to find a proper tension between rest and activity. Every time a family goes through a new change, even one as simple as the beginning of a new school calendar year, they will renegotiate how to express their priorities through the activities they choose to pursue. For families touched by disability, there is the increased challenge of incorporating many additional outside activities. These can include both frequent and varied types of medical appointments and therapies. When Timmy was a preschooler, we relocated to a region that had home-based therapeutic services. This simply meant that instead of attending a center-based program where Timmy would receive his occupational, speech, cognitive, and physical therapies, the clinicians visited him in our home. The good news was that Timmy received much more intensive, frequent, and personalized services than he had acquired in the group setting where he was previously enrolled. The bad news was that this arrangement created what we affectionately dubbed "The Parade of Therapists." Our entire life was dominated by a therapy schedule. If we weren't waiting for a therapist, working with a therapist, or wishing there wasn't a therapist, it was nap time, then dinner time, then bath time, then bed time. Somehow we were able to make a life in the midst of it, but the blessings of individualized therapy also created simultaneous complexities with time management.

Social Isolation

Every family has social connections of one sort or another. Some families are very well connected, while others choose a more reclusive lifestyle. For the family affected by disability, isolation is often an undesirable by-product. If a family member requires such constant care or supervision that it is difficult to leave the home, even grocery shopping may become an overwhelming task. When a family member has cognitive disabilities or mental health struggles, everyone involved might find social interactions to be more challenging and taxing. In addition, parents of children with disabilities have to work much harder at creating a social world for their children. Children with disabilities are often less likely to be included at the neighborhood birthday party or invited over to play after school.

When Timmy was a kindergartner at our local elementary school, there were three other neighborhood boys who attended kindergarten in the same classroom. One day, they all came bursting off the bus en masse, exploding with excitement about the birthday party they were about to attend for one of these little fellows. Exuding with the enthusiasm so typical of little boys at that age, they began to run up the road as fast as they could toward the birthday boy's home. Timmy did his best to keep up with them, going as fast as his short, low-muscle-toned legs would carry him. He too was elated at the prospects of a party! There was just one problem. He was the only one who was *not* invited. Several yards into his attempted sprint, I stooped down and enveloped his struggling form into my arms. It broke my heart to try to explain to him that he was not going, that he was not included. Although disappointed and confused, he was quickly distracted from the subject once we walked down the gravel lane to our house and entered the front door. I, on the other hand, felt like someone had seared my heart with a hot knife. Would it have been so difficult to invite one more child? Being excluded is an expected childhood experience from time to time. For children with disabilities, it is often much more common.

Access and Advocacy

Parents want their children to have access to opportunities in life and will work to provide those opportunities for them. In a family touched by disability, access to opportunities may be extremely limited while the energy required to advocate for family members may be enormous. It is simply a matter of proportion. A "typical" child may easily be able to join a local after-school community activity. A child who uses a wheelchair may be able to join the club, but may not be able to access the building because of its stairs. A "typical" child can be enrolled in the local public school, and the bus will automatically stop at his door to receive him. Despite the clarity of special education law, the parents of a child with special needs may have to justify why the school district should allow their child into their neighborhood school, advocate for the resources he needs, negotiate the components of his education, and bargain with the transportation department about providing him with a ride. On a different note, consider the situation at the average church. Is *everyone* genuinely welcome and able to attend the complete spectrum of programs at most churches?

For adults with disabilities, the access problems continue throughout life. Most adults expect to have the opportunity to contribute to society through the offering of their skills in the marketplace. Adults with disabilities often find significant barriers to meeting this expectation. While the Americans with Disabilities Act (ADA) has opened doors for people with disabilities, approximately 80 percent of adults with disabilities who remain unemployed would like to be working. Adults with disabilities who *are* employed are often *underemployed*, resulting in the loss of benefit packages taken for granted by others. In church settings, adults with disabilities regularly report that they are rarely considered for positions of leadership in their local churches, simply by virtue of the fact that they have some type of disabling condition.

Family Relationships

All families deal with constant minor adjustments in their relationships in order to find balance and unity in their family life. For families touched by disability, this can represent a larger challenge. Increased demands in every area of life can cause strain on relationships. Husband and wife may find it difficult to carve out time for each other, and when they do, they may find themselves empty of the emotional energy required to engage one another on a meaningful level. When difficult decision-making over educational or medical issues brings added pressure, this can create additional tension in the relationship. At the same time, when a husband and wife purposefully enter into these challenges as a partnership, they will often find deep fulfillment and an increased sense of connection in this shared bond that offsets the difficulties to some degree. It need not be a negative experience.

Both children of adults with disabilities and siblings of children with special needs can be blessed with unique opportunities while simultaneously burdened with unusual degrees of difficulty. Children who have disabled family members will often develop a more sensitive and caring approach to their involvement with others. They often seem to understand, experientially, a depth of compassion and human respect that is beyond their years.

When Freddy was ten years old he was invited to a birthday party for one of his classmates. After bowling together, the children were allowed to play games in the arcade inside the bowling alley. Being particularly skilled at one of the games, Freddy earned a significant number of prize tickets in the process. When the party was drawing to a close, my husband and Timmy arrived to take Freddy home. Freddy greeted Timmy by generously offering him all of his prize tickets. After pondering his prize options, Timmy chose a doll. In front of his fourth grade peers, Freddy approached the counter and purchased the doll and handed it to Timmy. Later, Fred remarked to me that it was incredible to watch. Recognizing that it was obviously a socially awkward situation for Freddy, he still did it cheerfully. First he offered Timmy all that he had. Then he allowed Timmy to exercise his own decision. Finally, he respected Timmy's choice— even when it potentially reflected negatively upon himself. Freddy demonstrated both generosity and respect beyond his years.

At the same time, children in a household touched by disability can become "lost in the shuffle" or required to accept responsibilities at an earlier age than their peers. All children need to learn responsibility as they mature, but children in families affected by disability generally exercise more responsibility *to* others in the family than they would otherwise be expected to do. If this drifts toward the extreme of requiring a child to feel and/or become responsible *for* others in the family system, it can cause distress.[3] Siblings or children of adults with disabilities need to have the freedom to experience their lives as *children*—not miniature adults—in the midst of their family situation. Parents must continually seek ways to be sensitive to the needs of their non-disabled children. These include time for outside interests of their own, the opportunity to constructively process their changing feelings about family life, and the need for a sense of God-honoring normalcy within the family system—a new normal. No one individual within the family system can live at that system's center, as that effectively becomes a form of idolatry, and results in spiritual and emotional ill-health for all of the family members involved.

The Results of the Realities

Families touched by disability experience the same types of challenges that other families face to adjust and adapt to changes in life. The difference is a difference of degree. Recognizing this fact makes it easier to relate to families who have disabled family members. At the same time, we need to realize that the cumulative effects of individual differences of degree can amount to a significant collective impact. How does this snowball effect manifest itself?

Stress

Every family experiences stress. Stress can be a positive and motivating factor in life. When stress becomes chronic or overwhelming, however, it can exact a toll. Families affected by disability experience magnified stress due to the multifaceted additional demands upon the family. Marriages can become strained. Non-disabled siblings may struggle under the weight of an increased level of responsibility within the family system. Embarrassment, self-consciousness, or fear may also increase a sibling's stress level.

In 2004, the results of a study on aging were reported in *The New York Times*. Focusing on mothers of children with disabilities as the research group, scientists evaluated the effects of a stress-filled lifestyle on the structure of their DNA compared to the DNA of mothers of children without disabilities. Upon examination, the mothers of children with special needs showed damage to their DNA that was potentially equivalent to a *ten-year-shorter* life span for these women.[4] That is an astounding result.

Exhaustion

Closely related to stress is exhaustion. Everyone becomes significantly fatigued from time to time. Often parents of young children feel chronically tired and inadequately rested. However, the long-term nature of the physical and emotional demands that accompany certain disabilities can drive caregivers to a state of utter exhaustion. When exhaustion sets in, but functioning must continue, the caregiver may sacrifice his or her physical, psychological, and spiritual health in the effort simply to survive.

The Remedies for the Realities and the Results

In the midst of their struggle to achieve a new normal life, families seeking to incorporate disability into their midst face certain realities involving personal care, education, behavior, time management, social isolation, access and advocacy, and family relationships. These realities have predictable results in the form of stress and exhaustion. What, then, are the remedies? And how can the church appropriately come alongside in a way that honors God, strengthens the family unit, and enriches the body of Christ?

Engagement

Families who are striving for a new sense of normalcy have significant—but not entirely unfamiliar—challenges to face. Often, the amount of energy required to make the adjustment results in certain activities being abandoned. Church attendance is frequently a casualty of this period in a family's life—one that, unfortunately, often drags on indefinitely. The statistics of unchurched families with disabled family members are staggering. There can be many reasons for this. Perhaps a family never regularly attended church prior to the entrance of disability into their lives, so for them, it is normal not to participate. Sometimes a family is wrestling with negotiating a path to acceptance. They may be questioning God's role in their lives, and church is the last place they *feel* like being at the moment. At times a family is exhausted, and the thought of advocating for access in yet another place—the church—is simply an overwhelming prospect. It is, frankly, easier to stay home.

Don't wait for families in this stage of adjustment to come to you. It is unlikely to happen. You will need to engage them, and you will need to do so "on their own turf." If you want to meet families affected by disability, try these options:

- Attend a disability-related support group in your community. Offer to provide child care at the meeting.
- Volunteer in an early intervention program or a special education classroom at your local elementary school.
- Attend the meetings of a disability advocacy agency in your county.
- Go to your local hospital and volunteer in the pediatric ward or at a rehabilitation program.

Recognize that families affected by disability often need your engagement in order to eventually become actively involved in the life of the church. Be where they are.

Boundaries

Once engaged with a particular family, how do you determine the appropriate level of involvement with them? This requires the prayerful discernment of boundaries on the part of the family and on the part of the church. Galatians 6:2–5 provides the biblical framework for making such an evaluation:

> *Carry each other's burdens* and in this way fulfill the law of Christ. If anyone thinks he is something when he is nothing, he deceives himself. Each one should test his own actions. Then he can take pride in himself, without comparing himself to somebody else, for *each one should carry his own load.*

Difficulties in life consist of two types according to this text: burdens and loads. As Henry Cloud and John Townsend discuss in their book, *Boundaries,* the first term is comparable to the idea of hauling a "boulder," while the second is comparable to the concept of carrying a "backpack."[5] This distinction is crucial in determining the level of specific involvement when coming alongside of a family adjusting to disability in their midst: "Problems arise when people act as if their 'boulders' are daily loads, and refuse help, or as if their 'daily loads' are boulders they shouldn't have to carry. The results of these two instances are either perpetual pain or irresponsibility."[6]

When a family is wrestling under the crushing weight of a boulder, it is essential that others actively and intensively assist in the shouldering of such a responsibility. However, if a family is struggling with learning how to carry its own backpack but well-meaning individuals step in and take the pack, this will ultimately harm the family and lengthen its struggle in learning to carry it as its own.[7] This does not mean that such a family will not need great encouragement and an abundance of practical assistance in its journey. But it does mean that there will be an appropriate level of struggle in building the family's "muscles" to operate under the increased weight.

Occasionally families in the process of building those muscles—just like Timmy did—will mistakenly believe that they are in the midst of a crisis that mandates 9-1-1 level intervention. This is not a time to be critical, but a time to be compassionate. When this situation occurs, there needs to be an honest evaluation on everyone's part. Is there really a crisis? If so, how can the church help lift the burden? If not, then how can the church stay engaged and supportive in a way that builds the family's muscles, while assisting and inspiring family members in the task?

Assistance

All families need help from others. That is one of the tremendous benefits of being a part of the covenant community of believers. Being the "hands and feet of Jesus" to a family with a disabled family member is a priceless gift. Very simple, very practical help can be extremely meaningful. Here are just a few examples:

- Deliver a hot meal on the evening of a long day of diagnostic medical testing.
- Provide respite care so a husband and wife can have a night "off" from the constant needs of their child with disabilities.
- Invite a child with special needs to come play with your children after school.
- Go once a week and feed lunch to an adult who has dementia, allowing his spouse to enjoy lunch out with a friend.
- Learn how to drive your friend's van with the wheelchair lift. Take the family member who is disabled to the mall to go shopping or to a sporting event.
- Stop by the family's home and take home a pile of ironing.

- Offer to accompany a parent to a medical appointment.
- For the family with frequent hospitalizations: Visit—visit—visit. Remember to keep your visits brief. Hospital stays are exhausting, and entertaining visitors for long periods of time can be taxing. Send money for parking and meals at the hospital.
- Volunteer to provide child care for siblings while parents attend medical appointments, therapy sessions, or school meetings with or on behalf of the child with the disability.
- Offer to do laundry and help clean the house.
- Provide a trained "buddy" so a child with a disability can attend Sunday school or youth group with his peers.
- Design a special event especially for a sibling to enjoy apart from the family member who has a disability.

Encouragement

Everyone needs to be encouraged. Encouraging one another is an important aspect of Christian living. "Therefore encourage one another and build each other up, just as in fact you are doing" (1 Thess. 5:11). Families that have experienced disability can be wonderfully uplifting to others. Recognizing the need so greatly themselves, they often demonstrate this gift to the church. Their experiences can uniquely equip them to speak genuinely and directly to the difficulties in others' lives. In addition, they sometimes unwittingly communicate encouragement through the examples of their own lives, which silently, but dramatically, model courage in the face of adversity.

In the same way, families affected by disability need to be recipients of encouragement too, and healthy doses of it! A little encouragement can provide tremendous motivation. It can be offered in many simple ways:

- Send an uplifting note.
- Make an affirming phone call.
- Stop and give a hug.
- Notice the hard-earned accomplishments of a child with a disability. Share your observations with his parents.
- Pay special attention to the siblings of a child with a disability, or to the children of an adult with a disability.
- Commit to praying regularly for the family. Ask for prayer requests and follow through.

Perspective

Losing perspective is a malady known to all of us. Scripture gives us the lenses through which to see with proper perspective. From time to time, all of us need someone to help us regain a balanced outlook in a situation. At times, families with a disabled family member will have a much better perspective on life. If they have done the hard work of negotiating a path to acceptance, they may have a clearer view of some of God's attributes, of what really matters in life, or of their own limitations.

In contrast, there will be occasions when they will be reeling from an onslaught of difficulties associated with disability that make it hard to see clearly. Life can become out of balance—the family's pie of life may become disproportionately sliced. They may begin to despair. If willing to answer the call, the church is uniquely equipped to come alongside of families struggling for perspective. The body of Christ can compassionately provide a biblically accurate focus for life. Grace gives us the freedom to be truth tellers about life as it really is, declare hope for the future, and testify to the character of God. At the same time, mercy is the vehicle by which we enter in and share in the sorrow, increasing our own perspective as well.

On occasion, professional Christian counseling may be warranted. Supportive individuals in the local congregation need to assess honestly when their ability to counsel a family effectively has been exhausted. The caring church will make it possible for a family to receive the services it genuinely needs by connecting them to a qualified Christian counselor and by assisting in covering the associated expenses.

Summary

The next time you encounter a family touched by disability that is learning to live a new normal life, will you declare an emergency and "dial 9-1-1" or will you see its struggles as extensions of your own? Will you ignore them in their challenges, or will you identify with the task before them? Remember: It's all different, and it's all the same. Families with a disabled family member face the same types of struggles as other families, but to a greater degree. May *all* families within the church be willing—in biblically boundaried ways—to engage each other by providing assistance, encouragement, and perspective.

Personal Application Questions

1. How does Featherstone's quote, "Differences differ only in degree from those of other families," help you to relate to the daily challenges of an individual or family touched by disability?

2. Have you ever found yourself passing judgment on the behavior of a child with a disability, or passing judgment on his or her parents? What do you need to change about your thinking in order to respond with compassion?

3. How can you proactively engage families affected by disability in your community?

4. Have you ever witnessed a family being crushed under the load of a "boulder" while the church stood by and watched? What was the end result for the family?

5. Have you ever witnessed "boulder vs. backpack" confusion in the church? What was the end result of such poor boundaries?

6. To whom can you reach out this week with practical expressions of assistance and encouragement?

9

On Grappling with the Great Opportunity

I run in the path of your commands, for you have set my heart free. —Psalm 119:32

It was barely six o'clock in the morning, and my body's transition from deep slumber to adrenaline-pumping shock was instantaneous. Before he'd finished the sentence, I was in midair, my eyes darting rapidly, searching for anything to wear besides my pajamas. "Steph, you need to get up. Timmy's not in the house," my calm husband, the ever-methodical-engineer, had whispered into my ear. "What do you *mean* he's not in the house?" I stammered in disbelief, hopping awkwardly into my jeans. "I've checked everywhere. He's not here. We need to go look for him," was the patient but concerned reply.

Since it was summertime, Fred jumped into his truck and sped up toward the local pool, knowing Timmy's love for water and his simultaneous lack of fear. I began running down the road in the opposite direction, wondering how long he had been gone, worrying about how far he had traveled, and pleading desperately for divine assistance and protection for Timmy. My prayers were answered in about thirty seconds. As I approached the end of our gravel lane that opened onto the paved street, eight-year-old Timmy rounded the corner. Not only was he a sight for sore eyes, he was a sight—period. Sporting an open backpack, he was wearing sandals, a baseball hat, his summer camp T-shirt, and . . . a pair of boxer shorts. Tim's greeting was a casual, pleasant, albeit slightly surprised, "Hi, Mom!" as in "Great to see you! What are *you* doing out here?"

Uncertain whether to be relieved or furious at this point, I articulated the question that begged for an answer, "Where have you *been*?" Even as the question escaped my lips, I noticed a videotape box in Timmy's hand with the name "Felak" written in black marker on the side. Responding to my own inquiry, I exclaimed, "You didn't walk all the way to the *Felak's* house, did you?" With apparent incredulity, Tim quickly replied, "Oh! No! No! No! . . . Well . . . I guess."

Further investigation revealed the rest of the story. Good friends from church, the Felak family lived in a home about a half mile away from us. Timmy had been there playing the day before and asked to borrow the video *Toy Story*. His request had been denied. Deciding to take events into his own hands, he arose early and hiked down the road to the Felak household. He walked in the front door, rifled his way through the video cabinet, located the prize, and headed back home. No one heard him. Guests were staying with the Felaks at the time, which meant that fourteen people were in the residence. Yet Tim's entrance, escapades, and exit all went unnoticed. He is a young man of many talents. More than that, the Felak children were chastised later that morning for watching television when they had been clearly advised the day before that the TV was off limits. The evidence was glaring. The videos were everywhere. But the exasperated denials persisted. Who would have thought . . . ?

During our conversation back at the Hubach household, Timmy realized that his parents were visibly upset. After explaining to him why we were so distraught about his disappearance, the magnitude of the dangers he had taken upon himself, and the importance of abiding by our requirements for him, we asked him if he understood. Nodding vigorously while bursting into tears he exclaimed, "You don't like *Toy Story!*"

As I clutched my head with both hands and my eyes bulged from the sockets, Timmy seemed to realize that, indeed, this was the wrong answer. I resisted the powerful urge to bang my forehead against a hard object. I took a deep breath and attempted to reinforce to Timmy that the movie itself was not the problem; the issue was that he put his desire to have it—his personal agenda—over his willingness to live in obedience to his parents' guidelines for him.

If we are honest, each of us must admit that we can identify with Timmy's experience when it comes to our relationship with God. We know what the clear and simple call of Jesus is to each of us: "Follow me." Yet, we also know what we want, which is . . . what *we* want. Due to our sinful natures, we struggle with valuing our autonomy more than we value our discipleship. And yet, by definition, the two cannot co-exist. One cannot be a half-disciple of Christ any more than Timmy could be half-obedient to his parents. Dietrich Bonhoeffer stated it this way in *The Cost of Discipleship*:

> Luther had taught that man cannot stand before God, however religious his works and ways may be, because at bottom he is always seeking his own interests. . . . When he spoke of grace, Luther always implied as a corollary that it cost him his own life, the life which was now for the first time subjected to the absolute obedience of Christ.[1]

So, what does obedience to Christ have to do with disability in the life of a family or an individual? One dimension of the lifelong struggle with grief that families and individuals touched by disability face is directly related to releasing *our* own agendas for our life in order to latch onto *God's* agenda for our life. Another dimension of the lifelong struggle with grief corresponds to the unwillingness of others to join us on the very journey to which the gospel calls *every* believer. The challenge of living with long-term disability presents a Great Opportunity in the life of a confessing Christian. It affords the opportunity to embrace the pathway of discipleship over the pathway of our own agendas, to identify with the Man of Sorrows, and to call others to this counter-cultural journey of faith.

Embracing the Pathway of Discipleship

All of us can identify with having agendas or plans in life. We are designed to be creative and productive, because it is part of the way in which we image our Creator.

> In Genesis, God gives what we might call the first job description: "Be fruitful and multiply and fill the earth and subdue it." The first phrase, "be fruitful and multiply," means to develop the social world: build families, churches, schools, cities, governments, laws. The second phrase, "subdue the earth," means to harness the natural world: plant crops, build bridges, design computers, compose music. This passage is sometimes called the Cultural Mandate because it tells us that our original purpose was to create cultures, build civilizations—nothing less.[2]

Recall that the cultural mandate was given in Genesis 1:28, prior to the fall: "Be fruitful and multiply and fill the earth and subdue it." The cultural mandate calls us to make plans, set goals, exercise the gifts that God has bestowed upon us, and experience the fulfillment of meaningful work. The underlying assumption of the *content* of the cultural mandate is that it is to be carried out implicitly in the *context* of the great commandment. Jesus summarized the Great Commandment succinctly when queried about the law by one of the teachers of the law. "The most important one," answered Jesus, "is this: 'Hear, O

Israel, The Lord our God, the Lord is one. Love the Lord your God with all your heart and with all your soul and with all your mind and with all your strength.' The second is this: 'Love you neighbor as yourself.' There is no commandment greater than these" (Mark 12:29–31). Our relationships with God and neighbor are so intertwined that Jesus presents them together as the Great Commandment. Old Testament scholar Gerard Van Groningen speaks of the original relationship between God and humankind as follows:

> God established a vital, binding relationship between himself and mankind when he created Adam in his image and likeness. . . . It was a bond that was to be expressed in a variety of ways. If the bond functioned as it was intended, that is, as an intimate fellowship with God and fellow men, and an obedient, devoted service with reference to the whole of creation, mankind would be blessed."[3]

However, the fall changed everything. While it did not negate the call to creativity and productivity, it had the real effect of dramatically altering the focus of mankind's energies. Instead of operating from a God-centered, relationship-based hub of creative and productive activity, we now struggle with an agenda-centered focus that reveals our underlying lust for personal control. We want our lives to be organized around our individual goals, while relationships to God and neighbor remain secondary—or, even worse, nonexistent. The problem with agendas is not necessarily the *content* of the agenda, although that can be an issue it is the *context* of the agenda. Scripture teaches that our goals and desires in life must always be informed by and subject to the Great Commandment—a relationship-centered basis for living. One major emphasis of the Bible's call to discipleship is nothing short of a radical call to embrace relationship-centered living as exemplified and empowered by Christ himself: first to God and then to neighbor.

The process of Christian discipleship could be defined as *dying unto self in order to be conformed to the character of Christ.* It is not the means by which we *receive* God's grace; it is to be our *response* to that lavish grace. The psalmist aptly summarized this concept when he declared, "I run in the path of your commands, for you have set my heart free" (Ps. 119:32). However, many twenty-first century confessing Christians live their lives blinded by the culture when it comes to seeing the pathway of discipleship. We live in an era of Big-Box Discount Store Christianity: an unlimited supply of grace offered at the lowest possible prices—guaranteed. Nearly eighty years ago Bonhoeffer warned of this phenomenon:

> Cheap grace is grace without discipleship, grace without the cross, grace without Jesus Christ, living and incarnate . . . . Costly grace is the gospel which must be sought again and again, the gift which must be asked for, the door at which a man must knock. Such grace is costly because it calls us to follow, and it is grace because it calls us to follow Jesus Christ. It is costly because it costs a man his life, and it is grace because it gives a man the only true life.[4]

What does this costly grace—the grace of discipleship—have to do with the reality of long-term disability in the life of a Christian family? The agenda-centered living to which each of us is easily lured is built on the pillars of ability and effort. It is an existence that builds ego based on what we are able to produce and accomplish in our own self-reliance. These agendas are not always task-oriented, but they are typically interwoven with the sometimes subtle, yet powerful, objectives of self-protection and/or self-promotion. What happens, though, when circumstances enter our lives—such as disability—that roadblock our way so that no amount of effort can advance our agenda, whatever it is? What happens when someone we love is laden not with ability but *disability*? It turns the worldly value system of agenda-centered living on its head. No longer able to shape our lives through effort and ability alone, and suddenly painfully aware that secular society's yardstick for measuring human value is woefully inadequate, we find that disability affords the Great Opportunity that God often uses to turn our faces gently away from our self-centered agendas and toward him.

At the same time, the extensive personal needs in the life of an individual facing long-term disability have a way of forcing us to refocus on the primacy of the relationship-centered life to which Christ calls us, and our woeful inadequacy for the task. But self-reliance finds its limits quickly in such an environment, and self-love is entirely incapable of providing for such great needs in the life of our "neighbor." Where can we turn? Recall from chapter 3 that respect-based relationships are built on the pillars of grace and the image of God. The relationship-centered life that loves God and neighbor is a life that finds acceptance in God's grace and radiates that grace to those in need around us. It is a life that finds its value in the image of God imparted to each of us—without regard for ability—and seeks to be restored to that image more and more by dying unto self and living unto Christ. It is a life empowered, not by self-will, but by the Spirit of God himself. We are faced with a clear choice: will we grope in the darkness, clutching to regain autonomy and retain our agendas? Or will we see what it is that God has for us to see—the starkly illuminated pathway of discipleship—the relationship-centered life that loves God most of all and neighbor immediately thereafter, empowered by his Spirit alone? Will we choose to pick up our cross and follow him?

Identifying with the Man of Sorrows

In Matthew 10:38–39 Jesus clearly states, "And anyone who does not take his cross and follow me is not worthy of me. Whoever finds his life will lose it, and whoever loses his life for my sake will find it." I once read the poignant account of a physician who was speaking with a family whose child had just been diagnosed with a significantly disabling condition. In that encounter the physician made the profound observation, "A child like this is a sacrament."[5] Upon considering the physician's words, the parents reflected:

> A sacrament is a partaking of the holy, the truth, the center .... To place it in the being of a helpless child . . . is to offer *an entirely different covenant with existence.* We saw our life and our child in a new light, not as a source of darkness or misery, but as in some way closer to truth and spirit.[6]

Christ calls each of us—not just those affected by disability—to an entirely different covenant with existence from that which our sinful nature craves. What is your covenant with existence? Is it to find your life, only to lose it? Or is it to lose your life, only to find it? This is one of the great paradoxes of the Christian faith: that losing is the only pathway to finding. And loss always involves a sense of grief, even when it reveals the road to true freedom and wholeness. In what ways do people touched by disability—or any of us, for that matter—experience grief when answering the call to genuine discipleship?

First of all, there is the grief that comes from releasing the agendas of our life even as we begin to grab hold of God's relationship-centered call to discipleship. Knowing that the pathway of discipleship is the best way is not enough. Many of us have intellectually assented to this truth all along. But coming to know it experientially—as a moment-by-moment act of faith and dying unto self—is a painful process. The death of our agendas is not a once-and-done experience. It is a lifelong battle in the process of our sanctification. As we die unto ourselves and live unto Christ, we will experience the process of being conformed to his image by cooperating with the transforming power of the Spirit. In Ephesians 4:22–24 Paul says, "You were taught, with regard to your former way of life, to put off your old self, which is being corrupted by its deceitful desires; to be made new in the attitude of your minds; and to put on the new self, created to be like God in true righteousness and holiness."

Before our son Timmy was even walking and while Freddy was just a preschooler, my husband Fred's employer approached us about moving to a new location in State College, Pennsylvania, several hours from our home in Ephrata. As a family, we had come through the rough waters of Timmy's infancy, had progressed in accepting the realities of his disabilities, and had begun to establish a new sense of normalcy. Just prior to the time we were asked to relocate, 40 percent of the engineers at Fred's company had been laid off. Considering the timing of this request, we were hesitant to decline the "invitation." Yet our lives were so fully invested in our friendships, in our church, and in Timmy's early intervention program, it was difficult even to entertain the concept of moving. However, we eventually agreed to relocate, and

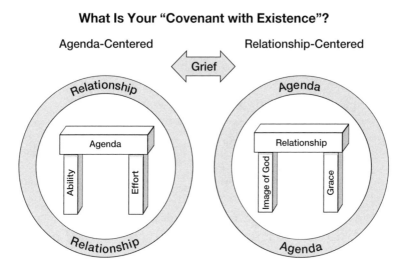

FIG. 2

What Is Your "Covenant with Existence"?

this move proved to be emotionally painful beyond my wildest expectations. The support system that had made our lives workable and enjoyable before was suddenly stripped away, and I felt trapped in the circumstances of my life. I wrestled with wanting my life back at every level: my sense of normalcy, my friends, my job, my church, and my dreams. I began to resent the parameters that framed my existence and the God who put them there.

Being solution-oriented to the core, I decided to take active steps to get my life back. I began to grasp forcefully for my latent agendas, only to my own frustration and intense disappointment. Intent on fulfilling my dream to earn a Ph.D. in economics, I enrolled as a full-time graduate student at Penn State University. Let's just say that the dream lasted about three weeks before I woke up again to the reality of the immense needs—many of them disability related—in my household. While I felt confident that my decision to withdraw from graduate school was in the best interest of my entire family, I still descended into a sense of deep loss and despair. Eventually, through the brave, gentle counsel of my long-suffering husband, I began to stop seeking solutions and start seeking God. During that time, in his grace, God exposed to me the idols of *my* heart and the goodness of *his*. I finally stopped asking myself "Who am I?" and began to focus instead on "*Whose* am I?" In his mercy, he pried my fingers off the agendas to which I held so tightly, and he illuminated to me the pathway of costly grace—the grace of discipleship. I had to lose my life to begin to find it, and although many grief-stricken tears were shed in the process, for me it was the beginning of a journey that has proved worthy of the struggle.

For many of us, there is also the lingering temptation to release one agenda only to grab onto another. While this phenomenon is not unique to Christians affected by disability, it can take on some unique expressions in the lives of people touched by disability. I know parents who have relinquished their coveted personal goals only to vehemently latch onto the agendas of disability rights and advocacy. I confess that I have been this type of parent at times. But switching agendas is not the call of Christ. The call of Christ is to submit all of our agendas to his Lordship—to live out the Great Commandment as the *context* of all of the *content* of our lives. In the work of access and advocacy for people with disabilities this means that we will always seek grace-based justice for the glory of God and for the good of every neighbor, not demand-based justice that seeks power and control for a select few. Our tendency toward what Paul labels "deceitful desires" implies that we must submit not only our activities but our motives to Christ's kingship in our lives.

There is a second way in which we experience a sense of grief when we begin to lose our life only to find it in discipleship to Christ. Recall that Christ is described by the prophet Isaiah as "a man of sorrows, and familiar with suffering" (Isa. 53:3b). I have often wondered if one particular way in which Jesus was a "man of sorrows" was in the grief he experienced when the call "follow me" fell on inattentive ears. Who better understood the truth and urgency of the gospel he proclaimed than Christ himself? And yet, "He was despised and rejected by men . . ." (Isa. 53:3a). Families and individuals touched by disability who begin to understand and embrace the pathway of discipleship experience great sorrow when others will not come along on the journey. Beginning to find their lives by losing them, they want others to know the richness of the experience, but the call often echoes back to them unanswered.

From time to time, my husband Fred and I have the privilege of speaking about disability ministry at churches or conferences. Once, when we were giving a presentation at a local church, an individual raised his hand at the end and defensively posited, "Well, this type of ministry is not for everyone. *It certainly is not for me.*" While we tried to gently affirm for him that not every individual is gifted to serve in every aspect of disability ministry, we did clearly communicate that every Christian is called to embrace people with disabilities into the body life of the church. He seemed to remain unconvinced. In that moment, it was as if our hearts were pierced, and we identified with Christ in his sufferings—as the Man of Sorrows. That encounter was an important reminder to Fred and me that we can present the call to discipleship, but only the Spirit can produce the awakening required for another to answer the call.

Calling Others on the Journey

Knowing that it is not within our control to convince others of the validity of an entirely different covenant with existence, why bother trying? Because in the very act of calling, the Great Commandment comes full circle once again. If we love God most of all, we will want to see his good and perfect will accomplished, and if we love our neighbors we will want God's very best for them—the abundant life. It has been said that "to love someone is to call them forth with the loudest and most insistent of calls to be all that God created them to be." The Scripture is very clear that none of us can even begin to experience all that God created us to be without being engaged in a restored and committed relationship to him. And that committed relationship means more than simply being recipients of his lavish grace; it also requires experiencing the costly grace of discipleship. These are two sides to the same coin of grace.

Perhaps you know an individual or family touched by disability that needs to experience this type of committed discipleship. They've gotten over the initial shock of disability, they're well along the road of acceptance, and maybe they've even begun to establish a new normal life. But they're shrinking from the pathway that is before them—the pathway of true Christian discipleship. How can you help? You can help by answering the call too.

When our family visited Disney World several years ago, we took our boys to a character breakfast where an assortment of Disney characters came and visited with the patrons. Timmy was particularly enamored by Mary Poppins at the time and lapsed into a dreamy-eyed state when she approached our table. After conversing with her and taking photographs, it came time for her to move on to the next family. Before departing, Mary Poppins offered to kiss Timmy on the cheek. Wavering about the ramifications of this, Timmy volunteered that she should kiss Freddy first, and then he would follow suit. Being the good sport that he is, Freddy participated in the plan—blushing under the prominent red lipstick marks on his cheek—only to be abandoned by Timmy when his own opportunity returned! Stunned and amused by Timmy's maneuver, we realized that he probably never had any intention of following through with the deal. How often do we treat other believers the same way when it comes to embracing the pathway of discipleship? "Go ahead . . . I'm right behind you." And yet, when they turn around, they find they have been forsaken and must make the journey in solitude. Answer the call too. Don't ask another to go alone. Discipleship that releases the primacy of personal agendas and embraces the relationship-centered life of Christ is not just the Great Opportunity for people touched by disability—it is the privilege and responsibility of every confessing Christian. It is not simply an individual call; it is a corporate call.

Alternatively, perhaps you are an individual whose life has been forever changed by long-term disability, and in his goodness, God has enabled you to experience the joy of responding to the appeal to "follow me" with intentionality and purpose. How can you help the church? By responding as Christ did, with truth and grace. Jesus stayed "on message" by expressing kingdom discipleship through story and illustration in many and varied ways. He always presented truth in a package that was designed for the benefit of his listeners—in a way that demonstrated love to neighbor. Jesus has given you a story through the word pictures of your life. Don't be afraid to share it. At the same time, always communicate the work of God in your life from a posture of grace. Being drawn from "clueless" to "committed" is a gracious work of the Spirit in anyone's life—never something that should be used to coerce another. Those around you need to hear truth with the forbearance and compassion that comes from a grace-transformed heart—one that understands that each of us is a work in progress—recognizing how little distance you have traveled down the road of obedience yourself.

Summary

In the Sermon on the Mount Jesus said, "Enter through the narrow gate. For wide is the gate and broad is the road that leads to destruction, and many enter through it. But small is the gate and narrow the road that leads to life, and only a few find it" (Matt. 7:13–14). Living with long-term disability can provide a Great Opportunity to illuminate the entrance to the narrow gate. It affords the opportunity to embrace the pathway of discipleship over the pathway of our own agendas, the opportunity to identify with the Man of Sorrows, and the opportunity to call others to this counter-cultural journey of faith. And when we deny ourselves and follow Christ—when we obediently cooperate with the Spirit to restore and conform us to his image—we are surprised to find that we become more fully ourselves than we ever dared imagine. Then we too can declare with the psalmist, "I run in the path of your commands, for you have set my heart free" (Ps. 119:32).

Personal Application Questions

1. What is your "covenant with existence"? What is the Great Opportunity that lies before each one of us?

2. Name the autonomous agendas in your life that distract you from a radical discipleship that loves God and neighbor most of all.

3. How does the presence of disability potentially provide a highlighted awareness of the call to God-honoring, relationship-centered living?

4. Why does the movement toward God-honoring, relationship-centered living result in grief for the one who moves? How can the church help?

5. In what ways can one pretend to be relationship-centered when, in reality, there is actually an agenda behind the relationship? How is such behavior dishonoring to God and disrespectful to one's neighbor?

PART 3

About Facilitation
in the Church

10

On Hospitality:
No Room at the Inn

While they were there, the time came for the baby to be born, and she gave birth to her firstborn, a son. She wrapped him in cloths and placed him in a manger, because there was no room for them at the inn. —Luke 2:6–7

As she relayed the story to me, I sat and listened in stunned disbelief. On the other end of the phone was one of my dearest friends from our days of living in State College. Barb's oldest son, David, was thirteen at the time we first met. Diagnosed at age two with severe autism* and intellectual disabilities, he required constant care and that care was a continual challenge that his entire family embraced with courage, faith, humor, and tears. Now he was a young adult living in a group home with several other young men who needed intensive supports. Releasing David to the care of others at the group home was a heart-wrenching transition for his weary parents who had loved him with such undying dedication, and yet, at the same time, it was a welcome relief.

---

* "Autism is a complex developmental disability that typically appears during the first three years of life and is the result of a neurological disorder that affects the normal functioning of the brain, impacting development in the areas of social interaction and communication skills. Both children and adults with autism typically show difficulties in verbal and non-verbal communication, social interactions, and leisure or play activities." (Source: Autism Society of America)

The first year had gone well—much better than they antic- ipated. And then the distressing phone call came. It was a staff person at the group home, several hours away from State College: "David's bleeding profusely from the mouth, and we can't figure out why!" Knowing that his medications had been changed recently, Barb quickly assessed that David had likely experienced a seizure and bitten his tongue in the process. After Barb urged the caregiver to seek immediate medical attention, the staff person quickly completed his conversation with Barb and then rushed David to the nearest hospital.

Upon David's being evaluated in the emergency room the physician's response was, "There's nothing I can do!" Translation: "We can't deal with *this!*" And he sent David home—in agony—still bleeding. No pain medication was given. There was no attempt to suture the tongue, and no antibiotics were offered. The doctor made no arrangements to seek counsel from, or organize transportation to, a larger medical center that might be better suited to address complex needs. Just "*leave.*" As a result of the lack of treatment, David developed severe blood poisoning, gangrene, and he lost one- third of his tongue. It took three weeks of hospitalization at another medical facility to remedy the effects of the emer- gency room physician's refusal.

When I heard this tale, a myriad of emotions swelled up within me. The hospital's response—so obviously inappro- priate and inhumane—engendered intense feelings of disbe- lief and indignation. "Isn't a hospital supposed to be a refuge of hospitality, a place of welcoming care for everyone in need of medical attention? How could *anyone* possibly do that to another human being in such apparent need?" And then it struck me: This story is an ugly but accurate parable of what we do—at times—in the church. Sometimes we forget that the church is not a country club for members, but a hospital for sinners of all different stripes,[1] with all different types of needs. And when we forget this, our response will probably be to shut the door: "Members Only. We can't deal with *this.*"

What does the Great Physician have to say about that?

> While Jesus was having dinner at Matthew's house, many
> tax collectors and "sinners" came and ate with him and
> his disciples. When the Pharisees saw this, they asked his
> disciples, "Why does your teacher eat with tax collectors
> and 'sinners'?"
>
> On hearing this Jesus said, "It is not the healthy who
> need a doctor, but the sick. But go and learn what this
> means: 'I desire mercy, not sacrifice.' For I have not come
> to call the righteous, but sinners." (Matt. 9:10–13)

The message of Jesus throughout the gospels is one of hospitality—without regard to degree of need or ability to repay. In
fact, his central point is that *every one of us* is in a state of dire
need and utterly, entirely unable to repay—but not all of us
realize this truth. In Jesus' explanation, the "righteous" are
not genuinely righteous; they just *think* they are. But the "sinners" are genuinely sinful, and they *know* they are. We each
need to recognize our neediness in order to embrace the hospitality that Jesus extends to us. The word hospitality means
"the love of a stranger." Though estranged from God in our
sin and brokenness, he pursues us with a love that is irre-
sistible. Love of a stranger. What a hospitable God we have,
and how desperately we need to learn to be more like him.

Statistics show that people with disabilities and their
families are significantly underrepresented in their involvement with the church. Many of these individuals express that
the church has been inhospitable to them either in attitude
or because of architecture, or both. Whatever the barrier,
the message—intentional or accidental—is not one of
"Welcome!" but one that implies "We can't deal with *this*."
How can we learn to model the Great Physician and help our
congregations to become more like welcoming hospitals for
sinners and less like exclusive country clubs? Jesus gives us a
clue in a passionate discourse about the Pharisees:

> Woe to you, teachers of the law and Pharisees, you hyp-
> ocrites! You give a tenth of your spices—mint, dill and
> cumin. But you have neglected the more important matters
> of the law—justice, mercy and faithfulness. You should
> have practiced the latter, without neglecting the former.
> You blind guides! You strain out a gnat but swallow a camel.
> (Matt. 23:23–24)

The essential characteristics of what the church is called to be—a hospital for sinners, as opposed to a country club for members only—can be found in this passage: justice, mercy, and faithfulness. Like a braided cord, a hospital for sinners could be characterized as a place where the love of a stranger is uniquely expressed through these three intertwined ways: the strand of justice, the strand of mercy, and the strand of faithfulness. Let's look at how these express themselves in ministering to and alongside of people touched by disability.

The Strand of Justice

For decades now, there has been a struggle in the realm of American Protestant Christianity—one that has torn the inseparable gospel into two distinct parts. In the twentieth-century battle over orthodoxy, the conservative church became guardians of the true gospel in word, while the liberal church claimed the territory of the true gospel in deed. Consequently, in evangelical circles, the mere mention of ministries of justice or mercy can be met with raised eyebrows. Yet the church must practice one without neglecting the other, for the true gospel in word and deed is one integrated gospel.

Throughout its pages, the Bible contains a staggering number of references to justice—more than two hundred times. Psalm 89:14 reads, "Righteousness and justice are the foundation of your throne; love and faithfulness go before you." According to this text, God's rule is built on righteousness and justice. Justice is very near to the heart of God, for it is one of the many qualities that the Scriptures ascribe to his character. As creatures made in his image, we glorify God when we reflect this attribute (or any other communicable divine attribute) back to him in whatever we do.

As Psalm 89 demonstrates, the concept of justice is integrally related to righteousness. Justice is the appropriate use of power to do what is morally right and fair. Leviticus 19:15 says, "Do not pervert justice; do not show partiality to the poor or favoritism to the great but judge your neighbor fairly." The "poor" in this passage could be understood to encompass the population of the disadvantaged in society. In contrast, the "great" are those with distinct economic or social advantage. It is significant to note that Scripture does not promote *compensation* of the "poor" at the expense of the "great," but calls for the *restoration* of a level playing field with regard to the treatment of both groups. The goal is not to show partiality to anyone, but fairness to all. This is a crucial concept to understand in ministries of justice for those touched by disability. When addressing disability in the church, the goal is not to convey that people with special needs are somehow God's special people—those who are due extraordinary rights and privileges. It is to restore a fair and respectful treatment of *every* person as a unique individual created in the image of God, including people with disabilities.

The antithesis of justice is oppression—the holding down of another—through the use of power in a way that is immoral and inequitable. Oppression can occur in any setting either actively or passively. Active oppression involves the intentional, immoral use of power against another person. In fact, a visual demonstration of an active oppression power play occurred at our house one Sunday morning. My husband Fred had left early in the morning to meet with a young adult in our congregation who has an intellectual disability. Fred was mentoring this individual through a church membership class specially designed to meet his needs. Meanwhile, back at home, I was attempting to rapidly apply my makeup before I had to quickly round up the troops to get to church on time. That's when Freddy burst upon the scene. Timmy had been playing with a new remote-controlled car that he had received as a gift for his birthday. This toy really was amazing. Designed to continue moving no matter what position the car was in, it would flip over and continue driving even when it ran into objects. I guess that's why Timmy thought it was safe to drive it down the middle of the street.

Upon his arrival, Freddy exclaimed, "Timmy's got his remote-controlled car in the road and he's determined to drive it all the way to church in front of the van!" Quite uncharacteristically, Freddy was showing greater regard for the preservation of the toy car than for the safety of his brother who, evidently, had already ventured into the street to place his car in the starting position. (Fortunately, we live on an unpaved lane that rarely sees any traffic.) After confirming the safety of Timmy's whereabouts, I asked Freddy to run out and carefully retrieve the toy vehicle. I quickly finished up and entered the garage, keys in hand.

Obviously exasperated, Freddy marched into the middle of the lane while Timmy watched the entire scenario from inside the van. As Freddy bent down to pick up the car, it suddenly lurched forward. Perplexed, he ran forward and reached again, only to have it race out of his reach. Reach, lunge, run . . . reach, lunge, run . . . huh? Suddenly, I realized what was going on. Timmy, with a determined glint in his eye—still holding the remote control in his hand—was using all of the power at his disposal to prevent Freddy from having access to his car. Nothing was going to change his plan—not if he could help it! Eventually Freddy successfully snagged the machine and triumphantly marched toward the house. The entire scenario was so ridiculous—and so hilarious— that I couldn't stop laughing on the way to church. Timmy's intentionality, Freddy's exasperation, and my initial cluelessness as to what was actually happening all converged together into another you-won't–believe-what-happened-at-our-house-this-morning story for me to share with Fred.

There was certainly nothing immoral about Timmy's antics, and his visual demonstration of the use of power was humorous, but it is a serious matter when genuine, intentional oppression occurs in the lives of human beings. Strong words describe God's response to such behavior: "Woe to those who make unjust laws, to those who issue oppressive decrees, to deprive the poor of their rights and withhold justice from the oppressed of my people . . ." (Isa. 10:1–2). Active oppression must never, ever be a part of the life of the church toward people with disabilities or any other individuals. It is entirely antithetical to justice—and completely inconsistent with the character of God.

But passive oppression can also occur, and this is more often the form of exclusion that takes place in churches. Passive oppression involves the holding down of another through what is *not* done—and it generally occurs due to neglect. Reasons for the neglect can vary along a spectrum from ignorance to indifference. Ignorance can result in a failure to provide due to lack of awareness that a problem exists, or because of an inability to know how to address a specific challenge. On the other extreme, neglect due to indifference is a complex matter of the heart: "We know, but we really don't care enough to act on it."

When a church building has a half-dozen steps to its front door and no alternative handicap-accessible entrance, it is quite literally holding down anyone who might desire to worship there but needs a ramp to enter. If a Sunday school program fails to address the Christian education needs of a child with Down syndrome in the congregation, and just looks the other way, it is holding back both that child and his parents from full participation in the body life of the church. When an adult with appropriate spiritual gifts is overlooked—*again*—for a position of church leadership simply because he is a paraplegic, he is being held down by his congregation.

Passive oppression, by definition, can be subtle, and we need to actively and prayerfully work at ridding our congregations of it in its many and varied expressions. It is easiest to confront when its root causes are ignorance because a little education can go a long way toward bringing about constructive change. However, the challenge is much greater when the crux of the matter is a congregation with cold, indifferent hearts—ones that God himself must warm and soften from within. When working with your church, please be cautious and do not attempt to judge the motives of the heart, for those are truly known only to God. Don't let the perceived callousness of others cause your own heart to become hard or self-righteous. Peaceful change comes about through a posture of humility. Perhaps you are sensitive to the holding down of those touched by disability, but your own heart is lukewarm toward those impacted by poverty, homelessness, or racial discrimination. Follow the admonition of Jesus: "First take the plank out of your eye, and then you will see clearly to remove the speck from your brother's eye" (Luke 6:42b).

At this juncture, a gentle word of exhortation is appropriate for church leadership: pastors, elders, and deacons. Throughout both the Old and New Testaments, the Scriptures demonstrate that responsibility for maintaining justice lies primarily at the feet of those who lead the people of God. If church leaders are not consistently preaching, promoting, and practicing justice, it will be nearly impossible for laypersons to encourage congregational change from within the body of Christ. However, when leaders boldly declare the Word of God on this issue, and set the example for the flock, God's Spirit can work in amazing ways—even in the hearts of the most indifferent in the pew.

Since every church is filled with sinners, any congregation will have room for improvement in the arena of justice. However, one of the key characteristics of a church that operates as a hospital for sinners is that it will demonstrate hospitality—the love of a stranger—through continually learning how to grow in exercising justice. In doing so, it will learn to identify and oppose all forms of active oppression, and be vigilantly self-reflective and repentant about passive oppression in its midst. The just church is an accessible hospital for sinners, open to all without regard to degree of need or ability to repay.

The Strand of Mercy

The second strand in the braided cord of what characterizes the church as a hospital for sinners, as opposed to a country club for members only, is the characteristic of mercy. When Jesus responded to the Pharisees' inquiry regarding his own hospitality toward sinners, he said: "But go and learn what this means: 'I desire mercy, and not sacrifice' . . ." (Matt. 9:13). What could he have meant by this?

At the core, the deepest difference between mercy and sacrifice is not just the outward expressions, but the motivations of the heart. In chapter 6, mercy was defined through the words of St. Gregory of Nyssa as "a voluntary sorrow which enjoins itself to the suffering of another." Simply put, mercy consists of a voluntary, engaged, personal relationship with someone in need. In stark contrast, the religious sacrifices of the Pharisees were part of a duty-driven, dispassionate, obligatory system that addressed their own needs. One who expresses genuine mercy is one who has experienced genuine grace. To experience genuine grace is to be conscious of our own brokenness, our helplessness, our utter inability to meet our greatest needs—and our absolute dependence on God who voluntarily engages us in a personal way. Only when we have come to the end of ourselves can we begin to find the One who empowers us to show genuine mercy to others.

A church that is characterized by mercy is a church whose service to others is voluntary, engaged, and personal. In other words, it is safe for the recipient. Because mercy is voluntary, the one who is on the receiving end of mercy knows that those who engage him are not doing so under coercion, but by choice. In Paul's second letter to the Corinthians, he writes,

> Each man should give what he has decided in his heart to give, not reluctantly or under compulsion, for God loves a cheerful giver. And God is able to make all grace abound to you, so that in all things at all times, having all that you need, you will abound in every good work. (2 Cor. 9:7–8)

Merciful service comes from a cheerful giver, and its engine is powered by the grace of God poured out in abundance. When people with disabilities, or any individuals for that matter, are served out of duty or obligation, then the service ceases to be mercy. And it becomes mere sacrifice.

Not only is mercy voluntary, but it is also engaged. Mercy doesn't stand on the sidelines and call out directions; it joins in the game and gets messy in the process. When we become actively involved in the challenges of another, we too will suffer. In his incarnation, Jesus intentionally identified with the struggles of fallen humanity, and in doing so, undertook tremendous pain in the process. Again, it is the apostle Paul who reminds us of how Christ's example of engagement applies to us:

> Your attitude should be the same as that of Christ Jesus:
>
> Who, being in very nature God,
>> did not consider equality with God something to be
>>> grasped,
> but made himself nothing,
>> taking the very nature of a servant,
>> being made in human likeness.
> And being found in appearance as a man,
>> he humbled himself
>> and became obedient to death—even death on a cross!
>>> (Phil. 2:5–8)

Engagement can ultimately be costly for the one who is showing mercy. This price is worth paying, however, because when our churches voluntarily engage others in mercy a safe haven is created for everyone. This safety is found in the caring assurance that no one is expected to wrestle with the challenges of life alone.

Finally, not only is mercy voluntary and engaged—it is personal. It is more than just voluntary service, although mercy involves voluntary service. It is more than engaging another at the level of their need, although mercy involves actively engaging a person's needs. Mercy also requires intentionally identifying with another in a personal relationship, one that is based upon mutual respect. Until the personal dimension of mercy is experienced, it is not yet mercy in its fullest expression. If our churches stay at the level of cheerful volunteerism through engaged programming, it is still possible to avoid genuine relationship. "Mercy is a voluntary sorrow which enjoins itself to the suffering of *another*." Not *others* in general—but *another*—a single, individual, unique, and precious person.

Several years ago, I was riding home in the car with Timmy. I was in the midst of working with a planning team to hold a Sanctity of Human Life service, and I had scheduled Timmy to read Psalm 121 along with Freddy that Sunday. So, I turned and asked Timmy if he would be willing to read the Bible for a worship service. This was his reply: "Sure! I know what it says: 'Jesus is King and he lives in our hearts. He loves you very, very much. Jesus knocks on the door and says, "Hey, Tim, can I come have dinner with you?" Then the boy, Tim, says, "Sure. I'd love to." ' " Timmy knows that the hospitality of Jesus in his life is deeply personal and it defines his understanding of the gospel. In a related way, a deeply personal form of service needs to define the church's expression of the gospel to others.

Keeping the manifestations of mercy personal helps prevent us from operating from a position of power. Recall that

Jesus "made himself nothing, taking the very nature of a servant." If the One who possesses all power and authority was willing to set that aside to relate to us personally, how can we do any less for others? Consider the following observation made by Leonard J. Vander Zee:

> But the difficulties and dangers of hospitality are not only in the guest, but also in the heart of the host. Providing hospitality can easily become a position of power over others. Being hospitable, we can subtly keep strangers in their place. I talked to someone who works in a soup kitchen. She said the hardest thing is to get the volunteers to sit and eat with the guests. Ladling the soup, handing out bread is powerful. Sitting to share it with the poor, the needy, the mentally ill, the ungrateful, makes us feel vulnerable. Will I be welcomed? Whenever we go to the Hope Rescue Mission, I always make a point never to work behind the counter, but to receive the food and eat with the guests. Sometimes I'm ignored; more often I'm profoundly welcomed and soon fall into conversations in which I learn more than I can ever teach. If we're always the host and never the guest, we lose our perspective, and we will fail to give others the dignity to welcome us.[2]

In its personal expression, mercy is a vulnerable experience for the giver that simultaneously imparts respect to the receiver. The result, again, is that such demonstrations of mercy are safe for the recipient. When the church operates as a true hospital for sinners, it recognizes that everyone has times when they are a patient, times when they are the Great Physician's assistant, and times when they are both. When we are mindful of this as the church engages people touched by disability in genuine mercy, we preserve their dignity, and ours. Wendy, an adult member of my home church, Reformed Presbyterian Church of Ephrata (RPC), relays her story as follows:

I am in a unique position to be both a Sunday school teacher of adults with special needs and an adult who sometimes has special needs. I have Sydenham's Chorea (SC), a disease where the immune system occasionally launches an attack on brain and heart cells, mistaking those cells for streptococcus bacteria, normally found in strep throat.

SC causes chorea (which is random, relatively rapid involuntary movement of all the muscles), tremors, and tics. Then SC short-circuits things like cognition, memory, emotions, behavior, and personality. These bouts can last anywhere from a couple of months to several years.

In 1996, I had my first bout of SC, and, in a matter of two days, went from being an independent, intelligent, professional young woman to becoming totally dependent, severely disabled, and scared out of my wits. As I write this, I am marking the first anniversary of my second bout of SC. As a veteran SC'er, this bout has been somewhat "easier" to deal with, because I knew what to expect. Nevertheless, I still needed lots of help this past year, and I owe a debt of gratitude to a multitude of people in my church, who have helped me through both of these rough periods.

When my SC was at its worst, I needed people to literally take over my life, because I couldn't do much of anything for myself. I did a personal "skills assessment" and was horrified to realize that the only thing I could successfully do was lie horizontally. Since it happened so suddenly, there was no time to get me admitted into any kind of nursing/rehab facility. And so, several families volunteered to take care of me until I could regain enough control over my muscles so that I could live unassisted. No one had any idea how long this would take when we made those arrangements, but they volunteered anyway. It took three weeks to get well enough to return to my home. Words cannot express my gratitude for those who made great sacrifices to take care of me.

Later on when I couldn't drive, people drove me to doctor's appointments. When I needed someone to transport home a chair that I had bought for physical therapy, someone took time out of their schedule to make it happen. When I couldn't afford to pay all my mounting medical bills, the deacons stepped in. When I had to give up teaching the adults with special needs Sunday school class, people substituted in my place. When I had to relearn simple things like numbers, people helped me by playing card games with me. I've received countless encouraging notes and know that there are lots of people praying for me. My church has made an indelible imprint for the Lord on my life.[3]

Listen carefully to Wendy's story. The hospital for sinners where she resides is learning how to exercise mercy that is voluntary, engaged, and personal. We are of course still imperfect, stumbling learners in the process, but the second strand of the braided cord that characterizes a hospital for sinners is being woven into place. Any church that has been grasped by grace can learn to do the same. Operating from a posture of grace, genuine mercy that is voluntary, engaged, and personal creates a safe, welcoming environment that duty-driven, dispassionate, obligatory sacrifice can't begin to imitate.

The Strand of Faithfulness

The final strand in the cord that characterizes the elements of a hospital for sinners is the strand of faithfulness. Ecclesiastes 4:12 reminds us that "a cord of three strands is not quickly broken." Bound tightly with justice and mercy, faithfulness gives the rope its ultimate strength. Faithfulness is the simplest concept of the three and yet, in many ways, the most difficult to fulfill. In differentiating between synonyms for this word, *The American Heritage Dictionary* states that "faithful in particular suggests long and undeviating attachment." In other words, faithfulness means unwavering, personal commitment for the duration. Repeatedly, the Scriptures remind us that God is faithful to his people. And, frequently, his faithfulness is mentioned in the same breath as his love. Consider the conclusion of Psalm 89:14: "Righteousness and justice are the foundation of your throne; *love and faithfulness go before you.*" And love "*always* protects, *always* trusts, *always* hopes, *always* perseveres. Love never fails" (1 Cor. 13:7–8a). "Always" is the epitome of unwavering commitment.

What does this mean for the expression of hospitality in the hospital for sinners? It means that the hospital for sinners is not a mobile clinic. It does not provide "hit and run" care. Holistic, long-term care that addresses the deepest needs of both body and soul is the work of the Great Physician, and it is to be our work, too. Remember from chapter 4 that "Disability is not like cancer. You can't get to the other side of it." When ministering to and alongside people touched by disability, this truth about the relentlessness of disability implies that the challenges these individuals and families face are here to stay. The life affected by disability is a marathon, not a sprint, and it requires the engagement of others who are willing to run the race alongside—mile marker, after mile marker, after mile marker.

But in the relentlessness of disability is also found a hidden gift, a potential measure of God-reliance that empowers the ability to "go the distance." Let us learn faithfulness borne of utter dependency on God—on his unwavering, personal commitment for the duration—from the example of our brothers and sisters in Christ who are experiencing disability. Many of them understand it at levels that the rest of us can only begin to imagine. As we follow their example, may we grow in our own dependence on God to demonstrate faithfulness in all of our relationships.

Summary

Let your imagination take you back to a night in Bethlehem, long ago. It is not difficult to speculate on what the innkeeper's thoughts were. After all, the streets were crowded, the guests demanding, the requests unrelenting. Then came the knock on the door, *again*. Now, standing before him was a young, pregnant woman whose eyes pleaded for a place to stay. "Ugh. We can't deal with *this*." And you know the rest of the story: "She wrapped him in cloths and placed him in a manger, because there was no room for them in the inn" (Luke 2:7). At his birth, the King of kings became the stranger who knew no hospitality. He identifies with those who know what it is like to be unwelcome. At the same time, in his ministry, Jesus the stranger was known for his dramatic demonstrations of hospitality—the love of a stranger. The church was never meant to be a country club for members only but a hospital for sinners—a refuge where the love of a stranger is uniquely expressed through the intertwining of justice, mercy, and faithfulness. May the day come when people with disabilities are not strangers to the church, but are welcomed into a community that offers justice in the form of access for all; mercy that is voluntary, engaged, and personal; and faithfulness that lovingly demonstrates unwavering commitment for the duration.

Personal Application Questions

1. How would you characterize your church—as a country club for members only, as a hospital for sinners, or as something else?

2. Which strand of the braided cord of justice, mercy, and faithfulness do you find most difficult to implement? Why? How can you rely on God's grace to express it?

3. Have you ever been the recipient of active oppression or passive oppression? How did you feel? Where is your church in need of acting justly on behalf of people with disabilities?

4. The expression of mercy is to be voluntary, engaged, and personal. Which expression is your church the strongest in exercising? Which expression is your church the weakest in exercising?

5. Does your congregation embrace faithfulness, or does it have a tendency to do "hit and run" ministry? What can you learn about faithfulness and God-reliance from people with disabilities in your midst?

11

On Belonging: Same Body, Different Parts

Just as each of us has one body with many members, and these members do not all have the same function, so in Christ we who are many form one body, and each member belongs to all the others. —Romans 12:4–5

Upon Timmy's entrance into the life of our family, I realized that many dimensions of my world would change. However, I did not anticipate that I would eventually develop such a friendly relationship with our local eyeglass practitioner. Most children and adults with Down syndrome experience a variety of different optical conditions that require correction through surgery or glasses. While I suspected that Timmy had vision problems when he was a toddler, I could not find an ophthalmologist who was effective at keeping him engaged long enough to acquire a reliable vision assessment. Finally, at age five, we found a steely physician whose authoritative command of his exam room yielded the rapid pronouncement, "This child has gross focusing problems." Prescription in hand, Timmy and I headed off to the optician's office for his first pair of glasses.

When it came to actually using his glasses, the physician's term "gross" must have imbedded deeply into

Timmy's psyche. In the first year, we found his eyewear in unimaginable places. It became so difficult to keep track of his glasses that I bought a red strap for them, not hoping that they would stay on, but hoping that I would at least be able to see them in the grass when he flung them off outside in the yard. Our immediate family and our close friends remember countless search-and-rescue missions for Timmy's specs. A repeated hiding place was in the downspouts of our house. Playing outside, Timmy would fold up the glasses and stuff them into the opening of the nearest spout. Once we found them rolled up into a little ball under the couch. On a different occasion, the entire extended family searched for an hour and a half on Thanksgiving Day only to discover that, all along, Timmy's glasses were inside the pocket of the shirt Fred was wearing—precisely where Timmy had placed them for safekeeping.

However, the most notable event was the time that we had given up the search in despair. An entire week had passed, and still, the glasses were not to be found anywhere. That is, until Fred came inside after doing yard work on a Saturday. "I found Timmy's glasses!" he stated triumphantly. "Great!" I replied, "Where did you find them?" "As they were flying out of the lawn mower chute!" he said, shaking his head, while offering the mangled, bright green pieces in his hand. Due to the extent of the damage, I began to feel distressed at the anticipated expense of replacing lenses *and* frames. Realizing that, once again, it was time to call my friend Gayle the optician, I picked up the phone and dialed. "Well, bring in the remains," she said, "there's always something we can salvage, even if it's just a nosepiece." Looking at the remnants I paused and replied, "I don't think so this time. . . ."

While it took time for Timmy to adapt to the *usefulness* of his glasses, the story was quite the opposite when it came to his adjusting to his *appearance* wearing glasses. Making funny faces in the mirror while he was being fitted for his first frames, Timmy was thrilled at the prospect of counting himself among the ranks of the bespectacled. So thrilled, in fact, that the day we arrived home with his new glasses he ran into the bathroom and stood in front of the vanity mirror. Mimicking the famous line from the story of Pinocchio, he cried, "I'm a REAL BOY now!"

In the story of Pinocchio, the central character shouted those memorable words, "I'm a REAL BOY now!" when he was transformed from a wooden puppet boy to a flesh-and-blood child. Why did Pinocchio consider himself to be a "real boy" when the magical change occurred? Now that he looked and acted like other children—he no longer perceived himself as "different." Unfortunately, the church's view of belonging is often similar to Pinocchio's. We think we belong when we blend into the religious crowd—when we are not perceived as different. Once, when I was traveling to a large denominational conference, I decided to entertain myself on the plane by trying to pick out the Presbyterians on board who were departing for the same destination. Sure enough, when I arrived at the conference registration table, I was right on the mark! Sometimes, as Christians, we fall into the trap of wearing the same type of clothes, reading the same type of books, using the same theological lingo, or assigning other similar markers that subtly identify us as belonging to the Christian community. But is this the biblical concept of belonging that is presented in the Scriptures? And how does the biblical concept of belonging practically manifest itself in the life of a congregation?

The Biblical Concept of Belonging: Unity in Diversity

Contrary to practices among many Christians, the biblical concept of belonging does not revolve around sameness. It rotates on the axis of unity in diversity. The apostle Paul stresses this theme in his epistles to the Romans

(Rom. 12:5–8), the Corinthians (1 Cor. 12:4–31), and the Ephesians (Eph. 4:1–16). Reflect on the following excerpts from these passages:

> Just as each of us has one body with many members, and these members do not all have the same function, so in Christ we who are many form one body, and each member belongs to all the others. (Rom. 12:4–5)

> The body is a unit, though it is made up of many parts; and though all its parts are many, they form one body. So it is with Christ. . . . But in fact God has arranged the parts in the body, every one of them, just as he wanted them to be. If they were all one part, where would the body be? As it is, there are many parts, but one body. (1 Cor. 12:12, 18–20)

> Make every effort to keep the unity of the Spirit through the bond of peace. There is one body and one Spirit—just as you were called to one hope when you were called—one Lord, one faith, one baptism; one God and Father of all, who is over all and through all and in all.

> But to each one of us grace has been given as Christ apportioned it. . . . It was he who gave some to be apostles, some to be prophets, some to be evangelists, and some to be pastors and teachers, to prepare God's people for works of service, so that the body of Christ may be built up until we all reach unity in the faith and in the knowledge of the Son of God and become mature, attaining to the whole measure of the fullness of Christ. (Eph. 4:3–7, 11–13)

Over and over again, the Scriptures stress that in our *unity* in Christ, we need to value and embrace the *uniqueness* of each individual. Consider the reflections of Jean Vanier, the founder of the L'Arche movement—a model of interdependent community living for people with disabilities and their non-disabled peers:

Community is not uniformity. There is a danger today, in our world, to want everybody to be the same, but then we lose our uniqueness. The incredible thing about us human beings is how unique each one of us is. The police know that, because of fingerprints. Each one of us, in every part of our body, is unique. There are no two people with the same fingerprints. Somebody calculated, in the realm of possibilities, how many real and potential fingerprints there could be since the creation of man and woman. I can tell you the zeros went a long, long way! But that means that I have to be seen as unique, as precious, as important, as valued. That is what a community is about—each person is seen as unique and has a gift to offer. Even the littlest and weakest person has a gift for the community, and that gift must be honored. Each one of us is very different one from the other. But all together we are like a symphony, an orchestra; all together we make up a beautiful bouquet of flowers. That means, however, that we must learn to love difference, to see it as a treasure and not a threat. Community means the respect and love of difference. Then we discover that this body which is community is the place of communion.[1]

At best, in many Christian circles, the uniqueness of each individual is tolerated—but not genuinely valued or embraced. This is one of the major barriers that families and individuals touched by disabilities face in attempting to experience meaningful inclusion in congregational life. Recall from chapter 10 that the church is called to extend hospitality—the love of a stranger—through justice, mercy, and faithfulness. While this is indeed the starting point, it is not, however, the ending point. Once welcomed into the Christian community, many who are affected by disability remain on the fringes—essentially living as strangers in the midst of all of the activity of the local church. The implicit message is, "Welcome! Come on in! But don't expect us to actually operate any differently because you are here."

Just as a family seeks to find a new normal life when disability arrives (recall chapter 8), the church seeks a state of new normal life when an individual who is disabled attempts to enter congregational life. Consider the following diagram of what often occurs. As you examine it, assume that "A" is a person with a disability desiring to integrate into the church and "B" is the current church community. The arrows represent accommodations that are being made. Three possible scenarios play themselves out.

The first scenario is the most common one. In this case, the current church community B expects person A to make all the adaptations so that the integration of person A is as effortless as possible for everyone who is already included in B. The problem is, this means that A must suppress something of what makes them unique in order to pretend to fit in, and in fact—if they have a permanent disability—will find it utterly impossible to do so. "Don't be who you are and you can be part of us." This approach is inherently disrespectful with regard to the value and uniqueness of person A, and minimizes the importance of person A in the body of Christ.

Fig. 3

Model of Belonging

C = Improved Inclusive Church Community

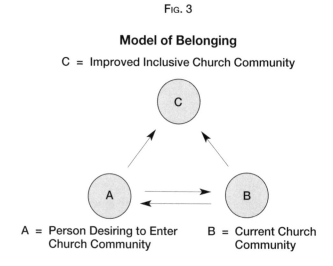

A = Person Desiring to Enter   B = Current Church
Church Community   Community

An alternative drama that occurs is when person A (or their family) expects the congregation B to incorporate this individual by implementing all of the idealistic adaptations that they propose. Such expectations often come with a demanding attitude and a hint of superiority. "Do everything I/we want and you'll be fortunate enough to have me/us as part of you." This approach is inherently disrespectful with regard to the value and uniqueness of the people in B and overinflates the value and importance of person A.

The third way—which is the biblical way—requires both parties to move to a wholly other and better place called "C." In essence, a new normal life is achieved for the congregation as it becomes an improved inclusive church community. In order to arrive at C, everyone needs to make some adaptations and everyone needs to be embraced for who they are. Unity is achieved while uniqueness is preserved and valued. A sense of corporate cooperation is exercised while the options of self-protection and self-promotion are rejected. The result is that the body of Christ is strengthened—it becomes *enabled* rather than *disabled*—a living picture of what Paul presents in the epistles. This can be hard work, but it is the work to which we are all called. And it is not optional. Listen to Paul's intense words:

> The eye cannot say to the hand, "I don't need you!" And the head cannot say to the feet, "I don't need you!" On the contrary, those parts of the body that seem to be weaker are indispensable, and the parts that we think are less honorable we treat with special honor. And the parts that are unpresentable are treated with special modesty, while our presentable parts need no special treatment. But God has combined the members of the body and has given greater honor to the parts that lacked it, so that there should be no division in the body, but that its parts should have equal concern for each other. If one part suffers, every part suffers with it; if one part is honored, every part rejoices with it. (1 Cor. 12:21–26)

This passage exhorts us to strive for *same body, different parts*—with every part expressing equal concern for the other—precisely what is exemplified by that wholly other and better place called C: the new normal life of the church.

Practical Manifestations of Belonging

The biblical concept of belonging revolves around unity in diversity, where equal concern is expressed for all the unique parts of the body of Christ. But how is belonging actually manifested in practical terms? When a church body is expressing a healthy sense of belonging, the individuals in that body will experience the gospel as a community through these five ways: *Christian education, community life, corporate worship, caring,* and *contribution.*

Christian Education

Christian education is the process by which we *hear the gospel* in ways that help us to understand it better. The gospel is not something we hear once, respond to, and move on. Each of us needs to hear the gospel over, and over, and over again. Every Christian needs the opportunity to grow in their faith through discipleship. Outside of instruction in the home, which is the primary source of discipleship for Christian children, Christian education is usually provided in structured contexts such as Sunday school programs, AWANA clubs, Pioneer Clubs, or youth groups. While organized group programs are the most *efficient* way to educate large numbers of children, they are not always the most *effective* way for all types of children. Some children don't learn well in highly-structured settings, while others don't learn well in highly-stimulating environments. In the group setting, the unique needs of the individual should be met in Christian education, while at the same time expressing concern for all of the members of the body of Christ. This means that belonging through having one's Christian education needs met will not always look the same for every child in every situation.

Whenever reasonable accommodations can be made to make an individual's participation possible in a typical setting, it is ideal to do so. For example, usually it does not take a special education major to teach a third grade Sunday school class that includes a child with Down syndrome, or learning disabilities,[*] or Asperger syndrome.[†] Often simple information on the specific disability, basic teacher training on learning styles, extra assistance in the classroom, and a hands-on approach to education is enough to bridge the gap. Fully inclusive arrangements for most children with disabilities are quite doable with a modest amount of effort.

However, a different approach might be necessary if a child struggles with significant behavioral issues. The goal of experiencing belonging through the vehicle of Christian education is to create a win-win learning environment for everyone. In this case, it might not be wise—or even possible—to attempt to incorporate that child into the entire instructional period of a typical classroom. But it might be very feasible to create a successful situation by encouraging that student's participation during singing or snack time while offering an individualized pull-out session for their personal discipleship. To foster a better sense of community for the child with

[*] "Students with learning disabilities (LD) have difficulty acquiring basic skills or academic content. Learning disabilities are characterized by intra-individual differences, usually in the form of a discrepancy between a student's ability and his or her achievement in areas such as reading, writing, mathematics, or speaking. . . . Intra-individual differences are differences within a student across academic areas. For example, a student with a LD may be quite successful in math computation and listening comprehension but may read poorly. Other students with LD may read and speak well but have difficulty expressing their thoughts in writing." (Source: Council for Exceptional Children, Division for Learning Disabilities)

[†] "Asperger syndrome (AS) is a developmental disorder that is characterized by limited interests or an unusual preoccupation with a particular subject to the exclusion of other activities. AS is an autism spectrum disorder (ASD), one of a distinct group of neurological conditions characterized by a greater or lesser degree of impairment in language and communication skills, as well as repetitive or restrictive patterns of thought and behavior." (Source: National Institute of Neurological Disorders and Stroke)

the behavioral disability during the pull-out time, reverse inclusion could be accomplished by inviting different children from the classroom to join the pull-out session on a rotating, individual basis.

When a large number of children with special learning needs attend the same church, an alternative option is to offer a distinct Sunday school class for children with intellectual disabilities. Christian education classes for children with special learning needs may enable the church to meet these children's unique requirements to hear the gospel in ways they can truly understand. Be aware, though, that separate classes can also diminish the sense of community with other children in the congregation. Creative ways of integrating activities between typical class settings and a special needs class can help to minimize this tendency. For example, groups could be combined to act out dramatizations of a Bible lesson from time to time instead of holding separate classes. It simply takes a commitment to building community across the entire group of children. The same principles apply if a separate Sunday school class for adults with special learning needs is established. No matter how Christian education is packaged, one of the ways that a child or an adult member of the covenant community experiences a sense of belonging in the body of Christ is by *hearing the gospel* through Christian education in terms that he or she can understand.

Community Life

Community life is the vehicle by which we *see the gospel* in the relationships around us. It is the three-dimensional picture that reminds us that we belong to the family of God—recipients of God's lavish grace upon us all. It is a place where we extend that grace to others and also experience it from their hands. For people with intellectual disabilities or mental health challenges, limited social skills can make participation in group social settings challenging. One way that our church has attempted to ease the level of difficulty for our adult members with intellectual disabilities has been to provide Friendship Families. Contrary to what the name seems to imply, the role of a Friendship Family is *not* to befriend the individual with the disability, but to serve as a liaison for that person: someone who assists them in making social connections and in meeting other families within the church. Of course, friendships naturally arise out of many of these relationships, but friendship is not something that can be assigned or orchestrated. It just happens. In our congregation, over the years, adults who have intellectual disabilities have become increasingly integrated into covenant community life. I often hear stories about hospitality extended for a meal at an individual's home on Sunday afternoon, dinner out at a restaurant with a church family, or invitations to enter into an extended family's Christmas or Thanksgiving celebrations. It is a beautiful thing. And it is a picture of the gospel expressed through belonging to the community life of the church—just one way we *see the gospel* in the family of God around us.

Corporate Worship

Another way that belonging is experienced in the church is through corporate worship. Corporate worship is, in part, our opportunity to *respond to the gospel* as a community. As one body with many parts, we come together to express praise, adoration, and thanksgiving for who God is and how he has worked in our lives. If we look around us, it is during worship that we often see unique and personal expressions of love for the One around whom we gather in unity. Some people will close their eyes, raise their hands, or sing with passion. Others may participate more quietly but sincerely, while yet others may pause and reflectively listen to the congregation in silence. For several years, our congregation had the privilege of worshiping with a young man with developmental disabilities who had a distinctive style of worship. Our family affectionately referred to him as William the Dancer.

William was an incredibly refreshing presence in the midst of a group of relatively restrained Presbyterians. When the music would start, so would William—in the front row. And his enthusiasm for praising God with everything in him was contagious to many. When William moved to another town and stopped attending our church, he left a noticeable void in our corporate worship.

When it comes to worship, we ought not to take coming before the throne of God lightly. As a result, I often receive inquiries from people on how to handle "disruptions" in the worship service. The crux of the matter is: how do we define a disruption? Just as "beauty is in the eye of the beholder," so "disruption is in the perspective of the observer." What might be a commotion or a distraction to one individual may actually be inspiring to another. I know—I'm a mom. One Sunday, Freddy was sitting next to me in church tapping his fingers rapidly on his hymnal. After this went on for quite some time, I cast a look of "cut that out" in his direction. He raised his eyebrows in surprise and whispered back, "What's wrong? I'm tapping a *godly* tune!"

In 1 Corinthians 12 Paul says we are to express equal concern for each other. It takes great forbearance for each of us to live with the idiosyncrasies of those around us. Before we are too quick to look for "alternative options" for another's worship, we need to ask ourselves the question: "Am I expressing equal concern for another, or am I only genuinely interested in my own worship experience?" If we are honest, typically we are less accepting of unique behaviors or diverse expressions of praise in a worship service than we ought to be. When a person with an intellectual disability sings loudly and off-key, is that a disruption or an expression of adoration? When an individual with obsessive behaviors cannot stop repetitively whispering, is that just cause for asking them to leave the sanctuary? The human soul was designed to worship. All people—even those with challenging behaviors—need the opportunity to experience at least *some* of the dimensions of corporate worship. We usually can find meaningful ways for that to happen when our focus is on expressing equal concern for one another.

Unfortunately, this does not mean that it is *always* possible for *every* person to be *fully* included in *every* aspect of corporate worship. If a person continually and loudly shouts through the entire sermon so that the pastor cannot be heard, equal concern is not being shown for all members of the body. One of the tragedies of life in a fallen world is that some individuals are so significantly impacted by behaviors associated with their disability that large-group community worship is not feasible for them or for their congregation. In such a case, instead of attempting inclusion in corporate worship, a small group of the body of Christ could meet with that individual to provide the opportunity to worship under conditions that are workable for the individual and the larger body of Christ. Such a solution would be a practical manifestation of showing equal concern for each other. If a person cannot go to the church, find ways to bring the church to the person.

Several years ago at a denominational conference, our senior minister, Pastor Tom, expressed his thoughts on "disruptions" this way:

> This ministry does require some flexibility. Sometimes when we sing, some of our members with special needs sway, or—horrors—even dance! Lots of Presbyterians don't like that, but we consider it a joy. Sometimes I hear the "clack, clack, clack" of seven-year-old Matthew's metal walker as he ambles down the aisle during the prelude. Some Presbyterians may not like that noise. But we remember when Matthew could hardly walk, and to us it is a joyful noise. God in his grace has taught our church that these are the kind of worshipers that Jesus seeks. "Let them come, and do not hinder them, for the kingdom of God belongs to such as these."[2]

Corporate worship is a tremendous privilege for the body of Christ. Making worship an experience of belonging, so that each unique person can *respond to the gospel* in unity—through praise, adoration, and thanksgiving—needs to be the goal of every congregation.

Caring

The means by which we *feel the gospel* in our lives is through caring. As Christians, we are called to care for our brothers and sisters in Christ and to accept their expressions of care in return. One day when I was serving in the nursery, a poster caught my attention. On it was picture of a boy who was gently placing a bandage on the arm of another boy. One of the two boys was in a wheelchair, and I was thrilled to see that the boy who was *giving* the bandage was seated in the wheelchair, not the boy who was *receiving* it. Often, we mistakenly see people with disabilities as consumers of our care but do not see ourselves as beneficiaries of their care. There is to be mutuality in the body of Christ in the giving and receiving of care, as each part of the body fulfills its unique function. When this interdependent exchange is taking place in the church between those with and without identifiable disabilities, it is a sign that belonging is taking place as we *feel the gospel's impact* together.

Contribution

Finally, we also experience belonging when we *extend the gospel* through contribution. Every member of the body of Christ has a contribution to make. All too often, when we focus on people with special needs, we emphasize their specific *disability* and fail to see their *abilities*. Of course, all people with disabilities have a variety of tangible abilities too. But Christians with disabilities are also fully endowed by God with spiritual gifts. Paul reminds us of this in 1 Corinthians 12:4–7:

There are different kinds of gifts, but the same Spirit. There are different kinds of service, but the same Lord. There are different kinds of working, but the same God works all of them in all men.

Now to each one the manifestation of the Spirit is given for the common good.

How differently would we view the giftedness of our brothers and sisters touched by disability if we remembered that "the same God works *all* of them in *all* men"? People with disabilities experience a significant barrier in contributing to the church when others fail to even expect them to possess spiritual gifts. As a result, those with disabilities are often overlooked for opportunities to contribute in meaningful ways to the life of the congregation.

Contributing to the body of Christ by expressing one's spiritual gifts can appear in ways that take us by surprise. The packaging of the gift at times causes us to miss it—or worse—dismiss it. Keith, an adult member of our congregation with Down syndrome, is a man with a mission—one that he executes with determination and grace. One evening the session was meeting in a glassed-in room in our church narthex. Keith saw them through the windows and walked right into the middle of the meeting. Looking each elder in the eye, Keith asked them his favorite question: "Do you love Jesus?" After hearing their replies in the affirmative, Keith reminded them, "Jesus is coming again." Then he left. Reflecting on that event, Pastor Tom remarked, "Now, you can look at that as an interruption or you can look at that as prophecy. God sent him to the elders of our church just to give us a check. . . . He comes in and says the most profound thing that could ever enter into a session meeting: 'Do you love Jesus? Is he the center of your life? Do you have the hope of his coming again?' " Adults with developmental disabilities regularly remind us that contribution comes in many forms, and giftedness can be presented in marvelously unique packages. Don't miss it—or worse—

dismiss it. Belonging is experienced through contributing—by *expressing the gospel*—using spiritual gifts "given for the common good."

Summary

In his heart of hearts, what was Timmy thinking when he looked in the mirror and declared, "I'm a REAL BOY now!"? Was he just mimicking a favorite line from a movie, or was he expressing a deeper longing of his soul? What would happen if the body of Christ paused to listen to the desire to belong that is so often part of the silent suffering experienced by individuals and families touched by disability? In contrast to the story of Pinocchio, the church needs to learn that sameness is not what brings a sense of belonging to the body of Christ. Instead, biblical belonging revolves around unity in diversity—a common oneness in Christ that values and embraces uniqueness in the individual. It is the reality of *same body, different parts*—where each part expresses equal concern for the other. And we can observe that genuine, biblical belonging is happening when the gospel is experienced by the entire covenant community in Christian education, community life, corporate worship, caring, and contribution. As the church increasingly practices biblical belonging, may the joyful shout of every congregation be "We're a REAL BODY now!"

Personal Application Questions

1. In your own words, how would you characterize the difference between "hospitality" and "belonging"?

2. Referring back to the A-B-C diagram on congregational inclusion, how does this dynamic take place every time a new person enters congregational life? Why is it more pronounced if that person happens to have disabilities?

3. There are five ways that the local body of Christ experiences the gospel as a community (Christian education, com-

munity life, corporate worship, caring, and contribution). Which one is your church most effective at promoting? Which one needs the most improvement?

4. Think about people in your congregation who have disabilities. In what ways does your church openly celebrate, embrace, and employ the gifts they bring to the body of Christ?

5. How does the body of Christ become *enabled* rather than *disabled* when any part expresses "equal concern for the other"?

12

On Wisdom: Questions Every Church Needs to Answer

*For the L*ORD *gives wisdom, and from his mouth come knowledge and understanding. . . . Then you will understand what is right and just and fair—every good path.*
—Proverbs 2:6, 9

Our senior minister, Pastor Tom, values the contribution of every member. Recently, he asked Timmy to assume the job of placing a fresh cup of water near the pulpit prior to the beginning of the worship service each Sunday morning. On one of the first Sundays that Timmy was to assume his new duty, he had already planted himself in his seat in the front row of the sanctuary. He was settled in, and had no intention of going to get Pastor Tom's cup of water. Not today. After I talked with Timmy, stressing the urgency of this task, he finally got up and huffed down the aisle toward the water fountain. He marched back in, put the water down, and flashed me a huge grin as he carefully placed the cup on the table. *How nice to see him come around so cheerfully*, I thought.

On the way home in the car, I affirmed Timmy for making such a good choice to change his attitude and fulfill his responsibilities. To this he responded, with characteristic transparency, "It was *hot* water." With simultaneous looks of shock and disbelief, Fred and I asked, "WHAT? You didn't give Pastor Tom *hot* water, did you?" Alarmed that it might have been boiling water from the coffee dispenser, we were at least relieved to find out that Timmy had retrieved the water from the spigot in the men's room!

In this situation, Timmy's response reminds us that ministry always has its challenges. Even when a church attempts to be hospitable and to promote a sense of belonging, unexpected difficulties will inevitably arise in effectively carrying out ministries of mercy and justice. Being committed to biblical principles is an essential starting place, but it takes wisdom to know how to implement those principles effectively in practice. If graciously engaging individuals and their families in justice, mercy, and faithfulness were straightforward, this chapter would be titled "On Rules: What Every Church Should Do." Instead, it is aptly titled, "On Wisdom: Questions Every Church Needs to Answer."

To better understand the dilemma before us, consider the following example from the Scriptures. One of the final and most sobering parables that Jesus taught prior to his crucifixion was the parable of the sheep and the goats. From the gospel of Matthew it reads:

> When the Son of Man comes in his glory, and all the angels with him, he will sit on his throne in heavenly glory. All the nations will be gathered before him, and he will separate the people one from another as a shepherd separates the sheep from the goats. He will put the sheep on his right and the goats on his left.
>
> Then the King will say to those on his right, "Come, you who are blessed by my Father; take your inheritance, the kingdom prepared for you since the creation of the world. For I was hungry and you gave me something to eat, I was thirsty and you gave me something to drink, I was a stranger and you invited me in. I needed

clothes and you clothed me, I was sick and you looked after me, I was in prison and you came to visit me."

Then the righteous will answer him, "Lord, when did we see you hungry and feed you, or thirsty and give you something to drink? When did we see you a stranger and invite you in, or needing clothes and clothe you? When did we see you sick or in prison and go to visit you?"

The King will reply, "I tell you the truth, whatever you did for one of the least of these brothers of mine, you did for me."

Then he will say to those on his left, "Depart from me, you who are cursed, into the eternal fire prepared for the devil and his angels. For I was hungry and you gave me nothing to eat, I was thirsty and you gave me nothing to drink. I was a stranger and you did not invite me in, I needed clothes and you did not clothe me, I was sick and in prison and you did not look after me."

They also will answer, "Lord, when did we see you hungry or thirsty or a stranger or needing clothes or sick or in prison, and did not help you?"

He will reply, "I tell you the truth, whatever you did not do for one of the least of these, you did not do for me."

Then they will go away to eternal punishment, but the righteous to eternal life. (Matt. 25:31–46)

The words of Jesus are stunningly simple in this discourse, yet carrying them out is complex at times. The parable reminds us that, if we are committed followers of Christ, we will extend grace and mercy to others in ways that naturally and concretely reflect our own personal experiences with God's grace and mercy toward us. Clearly, doing nothing on behalf of those in need is not an option for the disciple of Christ. Jesus' teaching mandates entering into the struggles of the hungry, the thirsty, the stranger, the naked, the sick, and the prisoner. At the same time, it takes wisdom to discern how to effectively and respectfully engage others in need. Where does such wisdom come from?

Proverbs tells us, "For the LORD gives wisdom, and from his mouth come knowledge and understanding. . . . Then you will understand what is right and just and fair—every good path" (Prov. 2:6, 9).

Tim Keller presented a series of lectures at the PCA Mercy Ministry conference in 2001. During his presentation entitled *The Practice of Mercy*, he stated the following:

> There's a series of practical policy issues . . . that when any church or any Christian group gets together and tries to work with people in need . . . these things come up. . . . And the only way to get from the theology to the skills is through these practical issues. . . . In your own particular work of mercy and justice you're going to have to figure this out.[1]

What are these practical issues that every church needs to wisely discern in the context of ministries of mercy and justice? According to Keller, they consist of the following:

- Whom do we help?
- How much do we help?
- When do we help?
- How do we help?
- From where do we help?
- With what attitude do we help?[2]

To explore these questions, the following sections will summarize Keller's assessment of biblical wisdom for each question, accompanied by disability ministry applications.

Whom Do We Help?

One of the first questions to arise in *deed* ministry is the question, "Whom do we help?" In other words, "Do we only come to the aid of those who are in extreme need or to anyone who is in need?" Keller quotes Puritan preacher Jonathan Edwards on this issue:

That we should relieve our neighbor only in extremity is not agreeable to the rule of loving our neighbor as ourselves. We are wont to be much concerned about our own difficulties before we meet extremity. Should we not be so concerned for our neighbor?[3]

When faced with many demands on our time and our resources, it is easy to fall into the trap of creating rigid rules by which we evaluate the needs of others. Keller urges that we resist this tendency. "The gospel and the golden rule suggest that we be very, very generous with our standard. Err, if anything, on the side of being too quick rather than too slow."[4]

Upon our becoming involved in the lives of people touched by disability, it rapidly becomes apparent that disability covers a huge spectrum. Disabilities can be cognitive, physical, sensory,* neurological,† or psychiatric in nature—or several of these disabilities in combination. Within these categories, there are abundant variations. Within those variations, there are differing degrees of severity. How does a church possibly go about addressing such diverse needs? Having a relationship-based ministry rather than a programmatic ministry is a starting place. If your church's approach to disability ministry is strictly programmatic, it will be quite impossible to develop specific programs that address the needs of every individual subgroup within the realm of disability. However, if your church approaches disability from a relational perspective, then programs simply become relationship-building tools to use when it makes sense to do so. For example, in our church, we designed our disability ministry to consist of five relational priorities. This does not mean that your church needs to construct its ministry in the same way. The essence of wisdom is discerning what is best in the context of a given situation. For the sake of illustration, we have found these priorities to be helpful:

---

* *Sensory disabilities* include deafness, blindness, or a severe vision or hearing impairment.

† *Neurological disabilities* result from damage to the central nervous system.

Facilitate the inclusion of people with disabilities into the body life of the church. The primary focus of our disability ministry is to provide the supports necessary to make inclusion in congregational life a reality. As a result, our special needs ministry does not operate as another category of ministry. Instead, we work *across* all of the existing ministries in the church. Every believer belongs in the body life of the church, and our special needs committee works with the ministries in the church to make that a reality. We have many people with disabilities for whom inclusion is already a reality. Their disabilities may not require substantive adaptations in order to make their participation happen, or those adaptations may already exist. For others, however, ongoing intentional facilitation is necessary. Our ministry focuses on such individuals. That does not mean that we minimize or ignore people whose disabilities do not require our efforts at facilitating their involvement. It simply means that we cannot focus on everything at one time. Our *focus* is on facilitation, but our *care* extends to anyone who has a need.

Educate the congregation on issues of disability in the context of ministry. To work effectively across the existing ministries of the church, ongoing education is necessary. We continue to be learners in this process, and as we better understand disability and how to effectively include people with disabilities in congregational life, we teach our congregation what we have learned. When I was in junior high, I received my Red Cross safety badge. I still remember the motto imprinted across the top of it. It said: "Knowledge Replaces Fear." Our special needs committee recognizes that most adults struggle with fear when first learning to relate to people with disabilities. Our purpose in educating is to facilitate meaningful ministry. Ministry happens through relationships, and relationships cannot flourish in an atmosphere of fear. By using a variety of educational tools that range from theological instruction to practical application, our congregation has learned that ministering to and alongside people with disabilities is the responsibility and joy of the entire church—not just a few "experts."

Guide small groups on how to provide appropriate support for adults with a disability or for families with a disabled family member. Our church body life is based on a small group model. Because of our size (about 350), members are encouraged to join a small group where significant, committed, caring relationships can be built. Our disability ministry's goal is to provide information, training, and ideas for small group leaders on how they can best address the disability-related needs they find in their groups. In addition to providing small group leaders with knowledge about specific disabilities, some examples of actions that might be considered include: Is the family receiving adequate respite care? Do the medical needs of the individual with special needs pose a financial hardship that the deacons could help alleviate? Are there transportation issues? Are there relational challenges that warrant intervention or increased support?

Several years ago, an article appeared in a well-known Christian magazine promoting the establishment of disability support groups in churches. The premise of the article was that families with like situations should get together for mutual support and encouragement so that their needs might be met. While it is true that families with similar circumstances will easily identify with one another, it is usually an inadequate model for providing tangible assistance. Since all of the families in the group share similar needs, the flexibility or the energy required to provide practical assistance is not typically available among the members. By integrating families touched by disability into the fabric of congregational life, there is a greater potential for significant care to take place.

Initiate Covenant Care Groups for families in extreme disability-related circumstances. Occasionally, the needs of a family are too immense to be addressed in the context of a typical small group ministry. One way that we respond mercifully to people affected by disability is to develop Covenant Care Groups for families, when appropriate. At Reformed Presbyterian, a Covenant Care Group is defined as "a covenantal relationship between a family in exceptionally difficult circumstances and a small group of church members who commit to assisting the family in the meeting of legitimate needs."

A Covenant Care Group has three main purposes. The first is to act as a link between the family and the pastoral staff. This allows the pastoral staff to remain fully abreast of the changing needs of the family without needing to stay directly involved on a daily basis. The second purpose is for the group to serve as a buffer between the family and the congregation. Curiosity and genuine concern on the part of congregational members can sometimes feel overwhelming to a family when it comes in the form of countless requests for information. The Covenant Care Group provides the family with a sense of privacy and normalcy by serving as a conduit for appropriate and relevant information. Finally, the Covenant Care Group mobilizes the congregation to provide emotional, physical, and spiritual support. By channeling the congregation's offers of assistance in concrete and organized ways, the Covenant Care Group allows the family to feel the caring presence of the church through effective ministry. Over the years we have started Covenant Care Groups for nine different families—some of them for families in extreme disability-related circumstances, some for people with life-threatening illnesses.

As recipients of the first Covenant Care Group at RPC, Patty and Roger Coiner are now leaders of this ministry. In 1988, their first son Douglas was born with multiple, significant medical issues. When Douglas was just twenty-two months old—still on oxygen and tube-fed—their second son was diagnosed in utero with even more complex medical challenges. Patty tells their story:

Samuel Roger Coiner was born November 24, 1990. Everyone from our Covenant Care Group was at the hospital with us. My husband and I were in considerable emotional pain and grief when our son lay dying in our arms. I can still feel his head lying softly snuggled against my shoulder as Roger and I lay in the two hospital beds that our Covenant Care Group had lovingly pulled together so we could share Samuel's last breaths. He died twelve hours later. There was no miracle in Samuel's physical body that occurred that night, but a miracle did take place in the form of God's grace, faithfulness, and almighty wisdom enveloping us.[5]

Covenant Care Groups become the hands of Jesus, touching the lives of those in our congregation who find themselves in extreme circumstances.

Promote outreach to people with disabilities. The final relational aspect of our disability ministry is to promote outreach. As noted earlier, our greatest priority as a congregation is to facilitate the inclusion of individuals and families who already identify themselves as part of the body of Christ. However, recognizing that the vast majority of people touched by disability still remain outside of the church, intentional outreach is also part of our mission. One of the vehicles that we use to promote outreach is a Community-Based Respite Care (CBRC) program. Working in partnership with a local disability service provider, our church has spearheaded a community effort to provide respite care services to families with elementary-aged children who have developmental disabilities. We offer fun, structured, thematic activities for children with disabilities and their siblings one Sunday afternoon per month at our church facility. Parents are then free to go out together, relax, and enjoy much-needed downtime with each other. CBRC provides us with the opportunity to show the love of Jesus to our neighbors in ways that meet very real, practical needs. Our hope is to draw families into the life of the local church where they can be introduced to Jesus Christ and ultimately experience both hospitality and belonging in his community.

Every church needs to ask itself, "Whom do we help?" when developing a ministry to individuals and families touched by disability. By focusing on relationships rather than programmatic structures, the church will be able to meet a wide variety of individual and family needs with a great degree of flexibility.

How Much Do We Help?

The essence of the question "How much do we help?" is "Will ministries of mercy and justice be a priority of the church, or will they be accomplished with leftover resources?" To be engaged in mercy ministry as an essential expression of the gospel is a costly endeavor. Keller states, "To bear burdens means some of the burden of the person you're helping falls on you. Until your help actually has an impact on you, you're not really helping. That is a hard saying."[6] Calling others to this form of sacrificial service requires great grace on the part of those who do the calling. "You, on the one hand, have got to show the church that this has to be a priority, it is a necessity, it is not an option, it needs to be done sacrificially. And yet, you have to show a kind of sacrificial, gracious attitude as you tell them about it. Otherwise, you are actually contradicting with your attitude and behavior the very attitude you want on their behalf toward the poor (disadvantaged)."[7]

Recently, I was driving Freddy to an appointment at the orthodontist. When I arrived at the office, all of the parking spots were full. Careful not to park in the only available slot—the handicap parking space—I squeezed my car into an area near the front door of the building. Freddy turned to me with a smile, and gently said, "You're not going to park *here* are you? Mom, I'm surprised. I thought you, of all people, would know better." I stammered at him, "Look! I didn't park in the handicap spot! I'm over here!" To this he replied, "Yes, but can't you see? *You're blocking the ramp.*" He was right! I was blocking the wheelchair ramp, and I was so intent on finding a parking space that I didn't even see it. Freddy's soft-spoken reminder made it easy for me to correct my mistake. It was masterful. Notice that Freddy didn't presume that I had an ill-motive. He was simply surprised that I failed to notice something of such significance, and gently but honestly brought it to my attention.

Calling your church to the priority of the ministry of mercy and justice to people touched by disability requires gentleness, sensitivity, and courage. Grace-based ministries need grace-based encouragement. Gentle redirection, an attitude that gives the benefit of the doubt, and the willingness to speak the truth in love are all necessary elements to God-honoring work in the church. The primary way that exhortation for change occurs is through the pulpit ministry in worship. For a lasting change of priorities to take place in church life, a foundation of solid, biblical teaching on mercy and justice needs to be built throughout the preaching ministry of the teaching pastor. A congregation must hear the call of the gospel *to* deed ministry before it will be effective at extending the gospel *through* deed ministry. Disability ministry, like any other expression of mercy and justice, must be an integral part of the work of the local church. Figuring out precisely how to lead your particular congregation to come to terms with that reality is a matter for prayerful discernment.

When Do We Help?

Of the six questions Keller poses, this one is, perhaps, the most controversial. At the heart of, "When do we help?" is the query, "Do we have standards or do we provide unrestricted aid?" Keller notes that the tension in this question arises from an ideological divide on the relationship between need and personal responsibility. Once again, Keller believes that the Scriptures call us to err on the side of generosity, just as God does in his dealings with us. "God starts with justification and then goes to sanctification. . . . He starts with essentially no strings attached and then expects that, 'If I am going to keep going with you and keep on working with you, you cooperate.' You have to be careful about coming in with a whole bunch of Pharisaical (rules), 'If you do all these things we'll start aiding you.' "[8] In the rare case that, after great patience and perseverance, it becomes apparent that the church needs to back down on the level of assistance, then, in the words of John Stott, "Make sure that mercy limits your mercy."[9] Taking vengeance out of frustration is never the appropriate Christian motive for withdrawing aid.[10]

How does this relate to ministry with individuals and families touched by disability? As discussed in chapter 8, it is essential that merciful relationships be well-boundaried relationships. The body of Christ has responsibilities *to* all of its members. All of its members are responsible *for* themselves and *for* their immediate families. When people encounter burdens that are beyond their ability to bear alone, they need the church to help shoulder the weight. Discernment is required to know when that lifting point should initially occur. Conversely, as the load lightens—or the family's ability to carry it strengthens—the time often arises when it is appropriate to shift more weight back in the other direction again.

One of the unique challenges that occurs in working with families touched by disability—particularly those with children who have disabilities—is that the church encounters the "entitlement mentality." Early intervention programs are government entitlement programs, meaning that children with developmental disabilities have legal rights to access certain services that promote their optimal development. Once children move into the public education setting, there are laws in place to ensure that they are not discriminated against in receiving services or in their attempts to be included in their district's educational environments. Just because these safeguards exist, however, does not mean that local agencies responsible for early intervention or public education always honor them. As a result, many parents learn to be quite vigilant about their children's rights and, at times, quite aggressive about securing services on behalf of their children.

The challenge in the church occurs when, often without realizing it, parents bring a demanding attitude to their local congregation. Even if the local body of Christ is attempting to engage the family with grace, the family itself may make the task quite daunting if they respond to the church with a demanding mindset. By developing a trusting relationship with the family, over time, the church can help to diminish this propensity. Gently and patiently, the local church needs to communicate the truth of 1 Corinthians 12:24b–25: "But God has combined the members of the body and has given greater honor to the parts that lacked it, so that there should be no division in the body, but that its parts should have *equal concern for each other*." When a family learns that it can trust its local congregation to show genuine concern, it will be easier for them to demonstrate concern to the church in return. Whether young or old—individuals and families who have been wounded in the public disability service system need the special grace and patience of their congregations. Let mercy be the only motivation that limits your involvement with them—not vengeance out of frustration.

How Do We Help?

When contemplating the question "How do we help?" the essential issue is "Can the church only get involved in mercy, or must it get involved in justice?" Keller begins his explanation by saying,

> The trouble with the word justice is, it sounds like—and it is—changing social systems. . . . You can't only do mercy. You're going to have to do justice. . . . You're going to find over and over again that individuals are imbedded in systems and unless you do something about them they're not going to get better.[II]

As discussed in chapter 10, ministries of mercy, justice, and faithfulness are the intertwining work of any hospital for sinners. And justice involves the uncomfortable work of confronting active or passive oppression—which is the holding down of another.

Disability ministry can be understood as a pro-life ministry in the fullest sense of the term. Engaging the lives of individuals and families who are touched by disability shows them that the church is *for* their lives—honoring the image of God in each and every person. Having a vision for special needs ministry that is deeply rooted in the sanctity of human life—in all of its diversity—can be quite energizing. When we realize that those upon whom God has stamped his indelible image are being trodden underfoot by dysfunctional social systems, it should stir our hearts to stamp out discrimination on their behalf. Many people with physical or sensory disabilities are quite effective at advocating for the rights of the disenfranchised in society, and there is much that we can learn from Christians with disabilities who are experienced in this arena. At the same time, many individuals with intellectual disabilities lack the power to be heard. Not only can the church be the hands and feet of Jesus on behalf of people with intellectual disabilities, but the church must be the *voice* of Jesus as well. For those individuals who do not have the ability or the power to be heard, others must respectfully step into the gap to speak boldly on their behalf.

One day, when Freddy was in junior high, we were having a conversation at the kitchen table after school. With a wry smile, Freddy remarked, "You know, sometimes people say, 'Fred, why don't you play football? You'd like football.' You know what I tell them? 'Black and blue aren't my colors.'" Getting involved in restoring justice to broken social systems is a lot like playing football. Many Christians bow out of the battleground for justice, claiming that "black and blue aren't my colors." But as chapter 5 explains, the gospel calls us to be agents of restoration bringing healing, help, and hope to the disadvantaged in society. The work of justice, through restoring broken social systems, is as much a work of the church as ministries of compassion. Every church needs to seriously reflect on how it is called to specifically carry out that work of justice itsown neighborhood and community.

From Where Do We Help?

The next question that every church needs to answer is, "From where do we help?" In the context of poverty, this question would examine, "Do we live in the places of need or do we commute there?" In responding to this inquiry, Keller quotes Bob Lupton, a pastor in Atlanta who is instrumental in leading ministries of mercy and justice. Lupton's comment was, "Programs do not restore community. Neighbors do."[12] Keller noted that if programs alone were sufficient to meet the needs of people, American poverty would have been virtually eliminated in the last thirty years.

In the context of disability, the question would be modified to ask, "Are we Sunday-oriented in our care for the individual or the family affected by disability, or are we all-of-life-oriented in our involvement with them?" It is easy to fall into the trap of compartmentalizing disability ministry into church-related tasks, such as providing an aide for Sunday school. But if we really understand the needs of families and individuals affected by disability, we will comprehend that what is often needed is a broader, more intentional involvement in their lives as a whole. This requirement, of course, is not unique to those touched by disability—it is the story of every human person. Meeting one's need for community cannot be neatly stuffed into programmatic time slots. Remember: "Programs do not restore community. Neighbors do." Who is your neighbor? Whose neighbor are you?

On one occasion, while I was visiting my friend Diane who lives at a local personal care home, a fellow named William—who has cognitive disabilities—approached the table where we were playing Scrabble. William, who is quite sociable, peppered Diane with questions about me. "Is she your case-worker?" "No," said Diane. "Your job coach?" "Noooo . . ." replied Diane. "Then why does she come and see you? How come you get to go out and do things with her?" "Because she is my *friend*," responded Diane patiently. "Your *friend*?" William said reflectively as he pondered this idea. "I'd like a friend! How do *I* get a friend?" Turning to me, he sincerely pleaded, "Can you find a friend for *me*?" If we limit our disability ministry involvement to what goes on within the confines of the church walls, we will miss the opportunity to minister to the Williams of the world. Every church needs to ask itself, "From where do we help?" Community-oriented outreach requires leaving the comfort zone of our church facilities and entering the daily world of others. It means being good neighbors—and friends.

With What Attitude Do We Help?

Several years ago, Timmy had an appointment with a physician who was a busy specialist. While we were waiting, Timmy was entertaining himself in the playroom with several other children. One of the girls in the room was a precocious little five-year-old. Attempting to make conversation, I asked her to tell me her name. To my simple question she replied in a loud and confident voice: "My name is Ramone! That's spelled R-A-M-O-N-E!" Smiling at such a dramatic presentation, I said, "Wow! You're a good speller!" At this point, Timmy turned around, cocked his head in my direction, and rolled his eyes. Out of the corner of his mouth he said, "How do you spell *pathetic?*" Timmy's reaction to Ramone exemplifies the judgmental attitude that resides, at times, in our own hearts. Every church needs to ask, "With what attitude do we help?" In other words, "Will the church engage people in need from a posture of respect or with an attitude of pity?"

Tim Keller describes the appropriate approach. "We have to go into any place of need expecting to learn from the people, expecting to be changed by the people, expecting to be a real servant of the people. . . . You have got to get rid of the pity and respect the people you're trying to help. Or you're really not going to be of any help."[13] Keller also notes that the attitude with which we engage others is a direct reflection of how deeply we genuinely embrace the gospel in our own lives. Keller continues

> I have to go in saying, "Look, do I believe the gospel of grace? Do I believe that what makes me right with God is not that I'm wiser and better and smarter? But that I'm just saved by grace?" Then, when I meet people, even people who don't believe like I do, I should expect—the gospel leads me to expect, the gospel alone of all the philosophies and religions of the world leads me to expect—people who differ with me in my beliefs might be better people than me; smarter people than me; wiser people than me.[14]

Where disability ministry is concerned, the worldview from which we engage people touched by disability will dramatically impact the way we respond. Recall from chapter 1 that there are three different perspectives of disability that are derived from our worldviews. Consider the following Worldview Perspectives of Disability and Their Consequences chart (see Figure 4). If we hang onto the historical view of disability that claims "disability is an *abnormal* part of life in a

Fig. 4

Worldview Perspectives of Disability and Their Consequences

Worldviews:	Historical (Modernism)	Postmodernism	Biblical
Perspectives of Disability:			
Disability is	Abnormal	Normal	Normal (expected)
The world is	Normal	Normal	Abnormal
General Summary of Worldview:			
The center of reality is	Man	Culture	God
Objective truth is	Knowable	Non-existent; "truth" is personal	Knowable and personal
Source of truth is	Science and reason	Pragmatic through "redescribing"	God Himself
Morality is	Relative (but uses borrowed capital)	Relative based on what "works"	Absolute
The overarching story is	Life is what we see and it can be fixed	There isn't one; not appropriate to "fix"	Creation/Fall/Redemption/ Consummation

Worldviews:	Historical (Modernism)	Postmodernism	Biblical
General Results of Worldview:			
View of self	Superior	Neutral	Valuable individual broken by the fall
View of people with disabilities	Inferior	Neutral	Valuable peer broken by the fall
Response to people with disabilities	Pity/Fear	No problem, so no response required	Identification
Responsibilities toward people with disabilities	Altruistic	Demands inclusion	Compassion, grace and justice
Relationship of community and people with disabilities	To fix differences	Demands sameness	Values differences and embraces inclusion
Family Responses per Worldview:			
View of compensation	Looking for it	Rejects it	Focus is on restoration of all things
View of compassion	Demands it	Offended by it	Embraces it and extends it
View of family situation	Envious of others	Denies existence of "problem"	Accepts challenges with perspective
View of assistance	Demands it	Demands sameness	Desires/demonstrates interdependence

normal world," we are likely to embrace an altruistic, pity-oriented response toward those with disabilities. Our reaction, conscious or not, will be "How do you spell *pathetic*?" Carrying around an overinflated view of ourselves and one that lacks genuine respect, we will likely create more harm than good as we condescend to the person who is, quite literally, the "object" of our ministry.

If, in contrast, we embrace the postmodern view of disability, which claims that "disability is a *normal* part of life in a *normal* world," we won't be motivated to become involved, because there really isn't any tension. If disability is a difference no different from hair color, then it really doesn't require anything of us. Rather than demonstrating respect by valuing the individuality of every person, our tendency will be to dismiss unique characteristics, unique gifts, and unique needs—instead, focusing only on similarities. The end result of ignoring differences will be to foster attitudes of *indifference*.

The biblical view of disability is, by far, the most respectful approach. It acknowledges the hard reality that "disability is a *normal* part of life in an *abnormal* world." As such, disability is essentially a more noticeable form of the brokenness that is common to the human experience. It is a difference of degree along a spectrum that contains difficulty all along its length. A biblical worldview promotes respectful identification with the individual touched by disability. From this perspective, we acknowledge that every person has not only needs to meet, but gifts to share. We also know that our value is inherently derived, not due to our gifts or in spite of our needs, but because we are image-bearers of the Creator. This means that we can, and should, expect to learn from people touched by disability—amazing things—profound things—beyond our own understanding or experience. It also implies that we ought to be slow to judge the parents of children affected by disability—realizing that we have not walked in their shoes. Wisdom is required to know how to relate to others in respectful and teachable ways. Every church needs to ponder the question, "With what attitude will *we* help?"

Summary

On that memorable Sunday when Timmy filled the pulpit cup with hot water, he could have found himself in proverbial hot water—had he not been dealing with such a wise pastor. When Pastor Tom saw Timmy the following week, he casually winked and said, "Hey, Tim! Thanks for the water. Next time, make it cold, would you?" Pastor Tom knows that Timmy has gifts to share with the church, but he doesn't expect perfection. He realizes that ministry to or alongside of *any* person presents unique challenges that require wisdom and discernment. Every church needs to seek wisdom from the Lord on how to best meet the needs of others: the hungry, the thirsty, the stranger, the naked, the sick, and the imprisoned. Every congregation needs to ask: Whom do we help? How much do we help? When do we help? How do we help? From where do we help? With what attitude do we help? Go ahead. Don't be afraid to ask the questions. "For the LORD gives wisdom, and from his mouth come knowledge and understanding . . . . Then you will understand what is right and just and fair—every good path" (Prov. 2:6, 9).

Personal Application Questions

1. What are some of the difficulties that your church has encountered in attempting to minister to and alongside people touched by disability?
2. Why does the diversity of the types of disabilities call for a relationship-based approach to disability ministry? Thinking back to the first section of this book, how does biblical theology inform this practice?

3. Are ministries of mercy and justice a priority of your local church? If not, how can you graciously and sacrificially call your fellow believers to this mission?

4. What is your church's collective attitude toward people with disabilities? Can you identify ways in which you need to "lose the pity"?

5. What are the dangers of the postmodern view of disability infiltrating the church? Why is the postmodern perspective an inappropriate replacement for the erroneous historical view?

13

On Change: Revolution or Reformation?

Knowledge is knowing; understanding is knowing what to do; wisdom is knowing what to do next; virtue is actually doing it. —Tristan Gylberd

Perhaps you've heard the expression, "Art imitates life." In our household the phrase could be more accurately stated, "Life imitates film." Timmy loves to watch videos, and often it is through making comparisons to film scenes that Timmy is best able to express his thoughts about life. He possesses an uncanny ability to memorize huge portions of dialogue and to recite each character's lines with recognizable and appropriate voice intonations, and his reflections vary from amusing to profound. Often, he will fixate on a particular film for a period of time, which means that, eventually, the rest of us weary of hearing about it.

Recently, the favorite flick has been not one film, but the entire *Star Wars* series. In addition to numerous dinner conversations about the complex relationships between *Star Wars* characters Luke Skywalker, Darth Vader, and Obi-Wan-Kenobi, Timmy has been overheard whispering to our dog, Ellie, "Beware of the power of the Dark Side." When I arrived to tuck him into bed one night, Timmy was hiding under the covers wearing a replica of the black mask belonging to the evil character Darth Vader—complete with voice modulating capacity. As I entered the room, he threw back the covers and attempted to frighten me with the notorious heavy breathing sounds of Darth Vader coming through the speakers of the helmet.

The most memorable *Star Wars* moment in our house occurred just last week. Timmy is the type of fellow who likes to "feel" his music. This does not present tremendous difficulties when we are at home, because he can listen to music in the privacy of his bedroom. In the car, however, the volume is never set where Timmy wishes it would be. If it rises to the level that Timmy desires, it doesn't stay there long before the driver insists on volume reduction. That driver is usually me. Last week was no exception. Upon entering the family van after a local shopping trip, I laid down the law. "If you touch the volume knob again, the stereo goes off until we get home." While obviously not too pleased with this decree, Timmy seemed to accept it nonetheless. That is, until I looked at him out of the corner of my eye. He was staring intently at the CD player. With his left arm lifted ever so slightly off his lap, his fingers were extended toward the volume control. While his hand hovered at least eighteen inches away from the controls, he began to turn his wrist back and forth with intentionality. I glanced at him and raised my eyebrows. "What are you doing?" Surprised that I'd noticed him, he said, "I'm using The Force to change the sound."

Do You Want to Change Your Church?

By the time you've arrived at this chapter of the book, hopefully one of two desirable options has occurred. Either you have become convicted of the need for your church to improve in the way it relates to people touched by disability, or—already convinced of the need—you now consider yourself better prepared to articulate a basic theology of disability, to communicate the issues that families face, and to cast a vision before your church leadership for your church's role in the lives of families with disabled family members. Being equipped with such knowledge and conviction can create a potentially precarious situation. If we are honest, many of us are like Timmy when it comes to altering circumstances with which we are unhappy. We may not attempt to access the invisible power source of The Force from *Star Wars*, but we do hope that we can somehow force change to occur in the face of undesirable situations. For many individuals and families touched by disability—and for those who love them and have come to understand their challenges—life in the local church can be an unpleasant experience. Perhaps there is not an adequate understanding of a biblical view of disability or a sincere commitment to respect-based relationships. Perhaps no one seems to understand the unique issues that individuals and families encounter in dealing with the onset or the relentlessness of disability. Perhaps there is not a prevailing attitude of hospitality and belonging. What then? In the face of such circumstances, how does one begin to promote constructive change in the body of Christ?

Revolution or Reformation?

Author and teacher George Grant once wrote a marvelous piece entitled *Revolution v. Reformation*. It beautifully embodies the essence of the dilemma that every Christian encounters upon attempting to be an agent of change either in the church or in culture. Here is a sampling of Grant's words on the subject:

> Like the way to perdition, the road to revolution is wide, and many are those who travel it. Like the road to paradise, the road to reformation is narrow, and few are those who travel it. It is little wonder then that men and nations actually prefer revolution to reformation. After all, the broad

road promises easy and efficient going. The narrow road promises only a long obedience in the same direction. The broad road advertises quick results, spectacular sights, and razzle-dazzle publicity. Whereas the narrow way offers only small beginnings, quiet faithfulness, and a humble reputation.[1]

Grant wisely discerns that revolution is the natural inclination of the human heart upon recognizing the obvious need for change. And yet, that inclination cannot be trusted. Why is that? Because at the center of our sinful hearts lies a lust for power and control. It is essentially the same struggle discussed in chapter 9—the tendency to choose agenda-centered living over relationship-centered living that loves God and neighbor most of all. We don't really want to build consensus—it is too hard and it takes too long. We don't really want to wait on God or others—we are too self-reliant and too impatient. We don't really want peaceful change—we want rapid results and we want them at virtually any price. Too often, the impulse toward revolution is energized by frustration, promotes the forcible change of external behaviors, values the attainment of its cause above the worth of others, and focuses on the acquisition of power from its enemies. What is available to the church when facing the overwhelming need for change in its midst? Is there only the price of revolution, or is there alternatively the promise of reformation?

The Biblical Model for Reformation

Fortunately, the Bible gives us a roadmap for peaceful transformation in Romans 12: reformation. In stark contrast to revolution, reformation is energized by God's mercy, promotes Spirit-led change from within the human heart, retains a sense of personal perspective while simultaneously valuing all people, and focuses on the expression of love toward others. At the center of the heart of reformation are

FIG. 5

The Differences between Revolution and Reformation

	Revolution	Reformation
Energized by	Frustration	God's mercy
Promotes	Forcible change of external behaviors	Spirit-led change from within the human heart
Values	The attainment of its cause above the worth of others	All people while retaining a sense of personal perspective
Focuses on	The acquisition of power from its enemies	The expression of love toward others

truth and grace, not power and control. As Grant states, the road to reformation is narrow, difficult, and humbling. Who would choose such a path? According to the writings of Paul, it is a choice that confronts every Christian. (See Figure 5.)

While it is certainly rewarding, the Christian life—when taken seriously—is also hard work. It is truly "a long obedience in the same direction." In the book of Romans, after employing the equivalent of eleven chapters to lay out God's plan for drawing a people unto himself, the apostle Paul begins to lay the groundwork for how the community of God's people should relate to each other. Indicating a significant tie-in with all he has previously stated, Paul begins his treatise on Christian living with a robust "Therefore, I urge you. . . ."

> Therefore, I urge you, brothers, in view of God's mercy, to offer your bodies as living sacrifices, holy and pleasing to God—this is your spiritual act of worship. Do not conform any longer to the pattern of this world, but be transformed by the renewing of your mind. Then you will be able to test and approve what God's will is—his good, pleasing and perfect will.
>
> For by the grace given me I say to every one of you: Do not think of yourself more highly than you ought, but rather think of yourself with sober judgment, in accordance with the measure of faith God has given you. Just as

each of us has one body with many members, and these members do not all have the same function, so in Christ we who are many form one body, and each member belongs to all the others. We have different gifts, according to the grace given us. If a man's gift is prophesying, let him use it in proportion to his faith. If it is serving, let him serve; if it is teaching, let him teach; if it is encouraging, let him encourage; if it is contributing to the needs of others, let him give generously; if it is leadership, let him govern diligently; if it is showing mercy, let him do it cheerfully.

Love must be sincere. Hate what is evil; cling to what is good. Be devoted to one another in brotherly love. Honor one another above yourselves. Never be lacking in zeal, but keep your spiritual fervor, serving the Lord. Be joyful in hope, patient in affliction, faithful in prayer. Share with God's people who are in need. Practice hospitality.

Bless those who persecute you; bless and do not curse. Rejoice with those who rejoice; mourn with those who mourn. Live in harmony with one another. Do not be proud, but be willing to associate with people of low position. Do not be conceited.

Do not repay anyone evil for evil. Be careful to do what is right in the eyes of everybody. If it is possible, as far as it depends on you, live at peace with everyone. Do not take revenge, my friends, but leave room for God's wrath, for it is written: "It is mine to avenge; I will repay," says the Lord. On the contrary:

"If your enemy is hungry, feed him;
if he is thirsty, give him something to drink.
In doing this, you will heap burning coals on his head."

Do not be overcome by evil, but overcome evil with good. (Rom. 12:1–21)

Listen to the weight of Paul's inspired words. The life of the Christian is a challenging one. It is the pathway of being "reformed and always reforming." How does Paul exhort us to bring about constructive, godly change—reformation—among the people of God? He tells us: 1) be energized by God's mercy, 2) follow God's pattern for renewal, 3) keep your perspective and remember your part, and 4) love others as God loves you.

Be Energized by God's Mercy

First, Paul urgently calls us to a sacrificial lifestyle when he clearly states, "Offer your bodies as living sacrifices" (Rom. 12:1). The very thought of sacrificial living causes us to cringe with discomfort. And worse than that, what Paul calls us to is *voluntary* sacrifice. When we offer our bodies as living sacrifices for God's kingdom, we voluntarily give of ourselves to a life of costly struggle, but we are motivated to heed the call "in view of God's mercy" (Rom. 12:1). God has engaged in "a voluntary sorrow which enjoins itself to the suffering" of his people. How can we do any less in return? When the Creator of the universe has condescended to present himself as a living sacrifice on our behalf, how can we not respond in kind with deep gratitude?

When we are tempted to become faint-hearted in the light of voluntary sacrifice, we can find great encouragement in remembering the life, and death, of Jesus himself. During his earthly ministry Jesus addressed the deepest need of people—their need for God—by first entering into the reality of their physical, social, or psychological struggles.[2] Jesus demonstrated diverse expressions of mercy in simply touching the leper, opening the eyes of the blind, feeding the five thousand, identifying with the woman at the well, and healing the paralytic whose friends lowered him through the roof. Jesus eventually gave the ultimate sacrifice on the cross in order to meet their need for God, fulfilling his own words, "Greater love has no one than this, that He lay down his life for his friends" (John 15:13). He continues to do the same for you, and for me. Touching our lives, restoring us from spiritual blindness, feeding our souls, identifying with our struggles, healing us from the paralysis of a life without God, and—having given ultimately of himself—interceding for us continually before the throne of grace. Living sacrificially, in view of God's mercy, is not about dusting off our Bibles and refreshing our memories about biblical events. It is about remembering the present reality of God's mercy—through Christ—in our individual lives moment by moment.

In order for us to be committed to bringing forth God-honoring change in and around us, we need to first be captivated by God's mercy *toward* us as individuals. Revolution is energized to promote change out of frustration. Reformation is energized to promote change as a heartfelt response of gratitude toward God for his merciful intervention in our own lives.

Follow God's Pattern for Renewal

Next, Paul reminds us that we need to follow God's pattern for renewal, not the blueprint of the surrounding culture. "Do not conform any longer to the pattern of this world, but be transformed by the renewing of your mind . . ." (Rom. 12:2). One of the most difficult truths about God's pattern for reformation is that the changes need to begin in our own minds first. Often when I teach a seminar on disability ministry, I can sense that there are people in the room who have come to find a way to fix someone else in their lives. "Tell me what I need to know to change my pastor." "I can't wait to find out how to show our Christian education director the right way to do this." Often, their expectations are altered in the first five minutes of the presentation, because Romans 12 teaches that transformation always begins with *me*. Transformation begins with the process of renewing *my* mind with God's truth and opening *my* heart to the work of the Holy Spirit to evoke *my* repentance and produce genuine change in *me*. Transformation is not something we can accomplish on behalf of others. We can be agents of the kingdom in the lives of others by graciously speaking God's truth to them so that their minds might potentially be renewed. But only those individuals can choose to receive that truth, engage it, and cooperate with it by God's Spirit.

In addition, reformation not only starts with me, but it is a continual process. We each need to be teachable about the areas of our minds and hearts that require ongoing transformation. Where does my thinking need to change? Where does the hardness of my own heart need to be softened? Where do I need to be seeking God in ways that I am not? It is so easy to focus on the ways we believe that others need to change and so easy to lose track of our own flaws.

As the possessor of a very competitive personality type, Timmy is notorious for hyper-focusing on the areas where he thinks Freddy requires improvement while simultaneously ignoring his own issues. One night there had been a significant amount of bickering between the boys at the dinner table because Timmy decided to play "manners police" with Freddy. This particular evening, the accusation was that Freddy had failed to put his napkin on his lap. Arguing back and forth ensued between the boys. Finally, I turned to Timmy and sternly said, "I don't want to hear *another word* about Freddy!" After remaining quiet for a moment, Timmy hesitantly embarked on a story. "Mommy went to the grocery store. She bought napkins. Then she set the table. Then, F-R-E-D-D-Y . . ." And Timmy proceeded to spell Freddy's name so that—technically—he was not actually talking about him. It doesn't take much imagination to identify with the parental frustration that Fred and I felt at this point. How much more exasperated does God become with our antics? God's pattern for reformation always starts with our own personal, ongoing transformation first. If we conform to the world's pattern—revolution—we will be prone to attempt to forcibly change the external behaviors of others. God's pattern for transformation—reformation—always starts with personal Spirit-led change from within the human heart. Such Spirit-led change is something with which we can cooperate, but not something that we can control for others. Speak the truth in love and let God do his work in your brother or sister—renewing the mind and transforming the heart—in his time.

Keep Your Perspective and Remember Your Part

Paul goes on to say, "For by the grace given me I say to every one of you: Do not think of yourself more highly than you ought, but rather think of yourself with sober judgment, in accordance with the measure of faith God has given you" (Rom. 12:3). Grace, sober judgment, and faith—these three in combination provide the prescription for perspective in life. When we recall that we are continually in dire need of God's grace, we will not lose perspective on ourselves. We will see ourselves through the lens of sober judgment and will rely on God's grace—through faith—to live with a sense of proper proportion as members of fallen but redeemed humanity.

However, if we approach the work of reformation in the church with an air of superiority or an attitude of arrogance, we will effectively throw huge roadblocks into the narrow pathway upon which we are calling others to tread. We will defy with our attitude the very principles we are asking others to follow. Such hypocrisy is not conducive to reformation, but a humble, proper perspective of oneself is. Remember, ministering to and alongside people touched by disability is not about creating a special class of privileged individuals in the kingdom of God. As chapter 10 explains, it is about restoring fair and respectful treatment of *every* person as a unique individual created in the image of God. What does this mean in practical terms when attempting to promote change on behalf of people with disabilities? It means that our approach toward others in the church—who may not yet appreciate the importance of this ministry—must still be bathed with grace and respect. Until Timmy was born, I did not even begin to remotely understand the significance of the principles described in this book. How can I condemn my brother in Christ who stands in the same place where I once stood? If I refuse to treat my sister in Christ with respect, but instead demand certain competencies from her first—only illuminating her shortcomings—then how can I ask her to focus on the goodness, truth and beauty in others? Each of us needs grace, sober judgment, and faith to maintain a proper perspective of ourselves.

Not only does reformation require keeping perspective about ourselves, but it also mandates remembering our part in the body of Christ. "Just as each of us has one body with many members, and these members do not all have the same function, so in Christ we who are many form one body, and each member belongs to all the others" (Rom. 12:4–5). Personal perspective and remembering our part in the body of Christ are closely related. If we think of ourselves more highly than we ought, then—by extension—we will also think less highly of others than we ought. Ministering to and alongside people touched by disability is certainly a significant responsibility of the church. At the same time, it is not the sole work of the church. God's people are also called to worship, evangelism, discipleship, outreach, and other expressions of devotion and obedience to Christ. Every church can and should have a relationship-based approach to disability ministry. But that will express itself in a myriad of different ways in the context of the other priorities of any congregation. Don't get caught in the trap of competing with the various ministries of your local church in order to prove "who is the greatest in the kingdom of heaven" (Matt. 18:1b). By respecting the importance of every ministry in our attitudes and our actions, we help to draw a living picture of the interdependence of the body of Christ.

American culture places significant value on personal independence. In this setting, it is easy to forget that as individuals in the church we play only a small part in the larger body of Christ locally, nationally, and worldwide. The gospel does not call the church to function as a disconnected entity of different causes for which we lobby. Instead, the gospel calls us to function as one harmonious organism that is God's agent for restoration in the world around us. And yet, we often forget our interdependence in the body of Christ. Remember: it is *same body, different parts*. Revolution is characterized by a loss of perspective that results in valuing the attainment of its cause above the worth of others. In stark contrast, reformation retains a sense of personal perspective while simultaneously valuing all people. Keep your perspective and remember your part in the body of Christ.

Love Others as God Loves You

Finally, and significantly, Paul spends the last half of the chapter addressing the subject of love. While it could be evaluated from different angles, one way of understanding Paul's passage on love is by looking at it as containing the categories of *sincere love*, *blessing love*, and *overcoming love*. All of us long desperately to richly experience real love from the hands of others. In reading through Romans 12:9–21, who wouldn't want to be loved this way? Truly, this is the desire of our hearts. And yet, we are called to extend this love, not to covet it for ourselves. Subconsciously, we often come to our circle of fellow believers with a set of unspoken, perfectionistic expectations about how others should love us. Such thinking denies the "already-not-yet-ness" of the kingdom of God as discussed in chapter 5. It inappropriately anticipates the experience of heaven here on earth at the hands of others, even as our own hearts are operating from a graceless and demanding posture. Recall that the kingdom is actually here in part, but we will not fully experience the restoration of all things until Christ returns to usher in the age to come. When we realize that the kingdom is only partially a present reality, it frees us up to gratefully receive the love that others are able to freely offer instead of always requiring more.

Much struggle ensues in the body of Christ when our focus is on wresting love *from* others, instead of sharing

Christ's love *with* others. This is a very difficult truth for individuals and families who are in need. It is so easy to approach the church with good intentions about reformation on behalf of people touched by disability, only to find our own neediness driving the agenda. The course can become easily skewed to a pathway that pursues "How do I bring about change so that I can get my needs met?" instead of "How can I be an agent of change by meeting the needs of others?"

Consider the text for the first category, *sincere love*, as demonstrated in Romans 12:9–13. Sincere love implies genuineness. How is this genuine expression of love described?

- It is honest in all things (v. 9).
- It is devoted in brotherly love (v. 10).
- It honors in showing respect (v. 10).
- It serves in zeal (v. 11).
- It is joyful in hope (v. 12).
- It is patient in affliction (v. 12).
- It is faithful in prayer (v. 12).
- It is generous in lifestyle (v. 13).

Straightforward and authentic in its expressions, sincere love reflects many of the multifaceted aspects of God's love. It is easy to see God's character displayed in the beautiful qualities listed above—rich and diverse. Consider how many of these characteristics touch on topics discussed in earlier chapters of this book: honesty (truth), devotion (identification), honor (respect-based relationships), service (how the church can help in practical ways), joyful hope (the most forward-looking expression of restoration), patience (the fruit of God-reliance in the face of relentlessness), faithful prayer (the most near-term vehicle of restoration in bringing healing), and generosity (the essence of a life touched by mercy and grace). The various manifestations of sincere love provide a marvelous pattern for wholeheartedly reforming relationships in the church.

In addition to sincere love, Paul also describes *blessing love* in Romans 12:14–16. According to *The American Heritage Dictionary*, one of the meanings of the word *blessing* is "to confer well-being or prosperity upon." How does this passage teach us to confer well-being on others through love?

- It is positive and courageous in the face of adversity (v. 14).
- It participates in another's reality (v. 15).
- It is harmonious in living (v. 16).
- It is humble in relationships (v. 16).

Blessing love is rooted in the awareness that God continually blesses us. He has been positive and courageous in the face of the adversity created by our fallen state, he has entered into our reality through the incarnation of Christ, he has brought harmony to our lives through the presence of his indwelling Spirit, and all of this has been accomplished in voluntary humility. In response to such undeserved mercy, we ought to seek to sacrificially confer blessings on others as well.

Timmy has an interesting perspective on God's desire to lavish his goodness upon us. One evening, about an hour prior to our scheduled dinnertime, we were driving past the local ice cream parlor. From the back seat of the van I heard Timmy call out, "Hey, Mom! How about some ice cream?" "No, not now. It's five o'clock. That's almost dinnertime," I responded. Undaunted by my answer, Timmy replied, "I'll ask God." Turning his eyes heavenward, he began to carry on a conversation with his Maker. "Hey, God! How about some ice cream? Um-hum. Uh-huh. Great!" Excitedly announcing the outcome of this dialogue, Timmy said, "Hey, Mom! He says we can!" While Timmy's genuine motivation was probably to get what he wanted, his statement still demonstrates to us his belief that God desires to bless us and those whose lives we touch. When we come to the church intent on blessing others from the abundance with which God has enriched our hearts, it is a powerful means of reformation.

The final type of love that Paul describes is *overcoming love*. This is the toughest type of love to express. It is a love that requires deep reliance on God in the midst of trying relationships or challenging circumstances. According to Romans 12:17–21, here are the characteristics of overcoming love:

- It is not vindictive in the face of evil (v. 17).
- It is righteous in the eyes of others (v. 17).
- It is boundaried in peacemaking (v. 18).
- It trusts in God's timing (v. 19).
- It employs God's goodness in victory over evil (v. 21).

Overcoming love loves in the face of opposition. It refuses to give in to hate, but instead chooses to trust God—that his ways are righteous, his timing is perfect, and his goodness is ultimately powerful. Our natural, fallen inclinations to revolution are most easily aroused in the face of adversity. Our innate passions will yearn to focus our energies on arresting power from those who are operating as our enemies. But God's prescription is for a different type of change—one that relies on *his* power—not the acquisition of personal power. It encourages us to appropriately influence what we can influence: our own righteous behavior and our own boundaries in peacemaking. But it also recognizes the limitations of human control and relies heavily on God's powerful love and perfect justice to triumph in the end.

Overcoming love is at the heart of reformation. Unlike revolution, which seeks to strip power from those who are operating as our enemies, reformation focuses on the expression of love toward others—a love that can only find its wellspring in God himself. *Sincere love* that is genuine and authentic, *blessing love* that confers benefit on another, *overcoming love* that loves in the face of adversity—these manifestations of love are the power of God for reformation.

A Personal Challenge from the Author

So which option will you choose? For your local church, will it be revolution or reformation? Revolution is energized by frustration, promotes the forcible change of external behaviors, values the attainment of its cause above the worth of others, and focuses on the acquisition of power from its enemies. But reformation is energized by God's mercy, promotes Spirit-led change from within the human heart, retains a sense of personal perspective while simultaneously valuing all people, and focuses on the expression of love toward others. Reformation: "the narrow road . . . a long obedience in the same direction . . . small beginnings, quiet faithfulness, and a humble reputation." Who would choose such a path? I hope you will.

One summer, when our family was vacationing at the beach, we visited a church where I learned a nineteenth-century hymn that had been unfamiliar to me. As I listened to the words, tears began to stream down my face. At that time we were engaged in a difficult conflict between the disability ministry and another ministry at our local church. Our two groups were at an impasse with each other over the inclusion of a person with intellectual disabilities. In my frustration, my natural desire was to "pull out all the stops" and start a revolution. In his grace, however, God used these words to inspire me to continue on the pathway of reformation. And it has made all the difference.

> O Master, let me walk with Thee
> In lowly paths of service free;
> Tell me Thy secret—help me bear
> The strain of toil, the fret of care.
>
> Help me the slow of heart to move
> By some clear, winning word of love;
> Teach me the wayward feet to stay,
> And guide them in the homeward way.

Teach me Thy patience: still with Thee
In closer, dearer, company,
In work that keeps faith sweet and strong,
In trust that triumphs over wrong.

In hope that sends a shining ray
Far down the future's broadening way,
In peace that only Thou canst give,
With Thee, O Master, let me live.[3]

Like Timmy's attempt to use The Force to turn up the volume, all of us will be tempted at times to employ force to evoke change in the face of undesirable circumstances. There is a better way: God's plan for peaceful transformation—the pathway of reformation. "Therefore, I urge you, brothers, in view of God's mercy, to offer your bodies as living sacrifices. . . ." Only through reformation will the body of Christ be made whole by enabling the full participation of people touched by disability in the life of the church. Holding fast to the biblical principle that all human beings have value and dignity because we are created in the image of God, may the church minister to and alongside people with differing abilities out of our deep understanding of our common need for grace. May the day come—and may it come soon—that we can sing with ever-increasing authenticity:

We are God's people, the chosen of the Lord,
Born of his Spirit, established by his Word;
Our cornerstone is Christ alone, and strong in him we stand:
O let us live transparently, and walk heart to heart and
        hand in hand.

We are God's loved ones, the Bride of Christ our Lord,
For we have known it, the love of God outpoured;
Now let us learn how to return the gift of love once giv'n:
O let us share each joy and care, and live with a zeal that
        pleases heav'n.

225

We are the Body of which the Lord is Head,
Called to obey him, now risen from the dead;
He wills us be a family, diverse yet truly one:
O let us give our gifts to God, and so shall his work on
    earth be done.

We are a temple, the Spirit's dwelling place,
Formed in great weakness, a cup to hold God's grace;
We die alone, for on its own each member loses fire:
Yet joined in one the flame burns on to give warmth and
    light, and to inspire.[4]

And all God's people said, "Amen."

Personal Application Questions

1. When it comes to your church's approach to people touched by disability, where is your personal frustration level on a scale of 1 to 10?

2. In your own words, describe the difference between revolution and reformation.

3. Why does revolution seem to be the easiest pathway when one feels frustrated?

4. Why is reformation so challenging and yet so promising?

5. If you've already started down the road to revolution, how will you change your course?

6. If you've never started down the pathway to reformation, how will you begin today? What specific steps will you take?

Notes

Chapter 1: On Truth: The Four Missing Words

1. Cesar Franck, "O, Lord Most Holy (Panis Angelicus)" (Milwaukee: G. Schirmer Inc., Distributed by Hal Leonard Corporation, n.d.).

2. Norman Kunc and Emma Van der Klift, "Credo for Support," http://normemma.com/credopos.htm, (January 24, 2004).

3. Carol Tashdie and Zach Rosetti, "Facilitating Friendship: Barriers and Strategies" (unpublished paper presented at National Down Syndrome Conference, Philadelphia, August 2003), 2.

4. Francis A. Schaeffer, *The God Who Is There, 30th Anniversary edition* (Downers Grove, IL: InterVarsity Press, 1998), 132.

Chapter 2: On Identification: Same Lake, Different Boat

1. Gerard Van Groningen, *Messianic Revelation in the Old Testament*, vol. 1 (Eugene, OR: Wipf and Stock, 1997), 59–60.

2. Ibid., 103.

Chapter 3: On Respect: Common Grace, Special Needs

1. Jerram Barrs, "Lecture 17 Acts: A Challenge to Mission Part 5," *Apologetics and Outreach to Contemporary Culture* video. (St. Louis: Covenant Theological Seminary, 2001)

2. Paige Benton, "Session 1: Grace Saves Us," *Fruit of Grace Conference* video. (Denver: PCA, September 2001)

3. Barrs, "Lecture 17 Acts: A Challenge to Mission Part 5," *Apologetics and Outreach to Contemporary Culture*, video.

Chapter 4: On Relentlessness: Dante's Circles of Disability

1. Helen Featherstone, *A Difference in the Family* (New York: Penguin Books, 1981), 12.

Chapter 5: On Restoration: Thy Kingdom Come

1. Timothy J. Keller, *Ministries of Mercy: The Call of the Jericho Road* (Phillipsburg, NJ: P&R, 1997), 52–53.

2. Ibid., 52.

3. Herman Ridderbos, *The Coming of the Kingdom* (Phillipsburg, NJ: P&R, 1962), 186.

4. Chuck Colson, *Kingdoms in Conflict* (Grand Rapids: Zondervan, 1989), 86.

5. Francis Schaeffer, *The God Who Is There* (Downers Grove, IL: InterVarsity Press, 1982), 188.

6. George Eldon Ladd, *A Theology of the New Testament* (Grand Rapids: Eerdmans, 1993), 101.

7. Timothy J. Keller, "Session 1: The Upside Down Kingdom," *Sharing Christ, Showing Mercy Conference* video. (Atlanta: PCA, March 2001)

Chapter 6: On Coming to Terms with a New Reality

1. Elisabeth Kubler-Ross, *On Death and Dying* (New York: Touchstone, 1969), 9.

2. Joni Eareckson Tada, "General Session One," *1999 International Women in the Church Conference* video. (Atlanta: PCA, 1999)

Chapter 7: On Negotiating a Path to Acceptance

1. M. Scott Peck, *The Road Less Traveled: A New Psychology of Love, Traditional Values and Spiritual Growth* (New York: Simon and Schuster, 1978), 15.

2. Christopher de Vinck, *The Power of the Powerless* (Grand Rapids: Zondervan, 1988), 28.

3. Ibid., 31–32.

4. Samuel Rodigast, "Whate'er My God Ordains Is Right," *Trinity Hymnal* (Atlanta: Great Commission Publications, 1990), No. 108.

5. Horatio G. Spafford, "It Is Well with My Soul," *Trinity Hymnal* (Atlanta: Great Commission Publications, 1990), No. 691.

Chapter 8: On Living a New Normal Life

1. Helen Featherstone, *A Difference in the Family* (New York: Penguin Books, 1981), 12.

2. "Promise Christian Academy Philosophy of Education," http://kirkofthehills.org/pca/philosophy.htm, (November 21 , 2005).

3. Henry Cloud and John Townsend, *Boundaries*. (Grand Rapids: Zondervan, 1992), 30.

4. Benedict Carey, "Stress and Distress May Give Your Genes Gray Hair," *The New York Times* (November 30 , 2004), D5.

5. Cloud and Townsend, *Boundaries*, 31.

6. Ibid., 31.

7. Ibid., 31–32.

Chapter 9: On Grappling with the Great Opportunity

1. Dietrich Bonhoeffer, *The Cost of Discipleship* (New York: MacMillan, 1963), 53.

2. Nancy Pearcey, *Total Truth: Liberating Christianity from Its Cultural Captivity* (Wheaton, IL: Crossway, 2004), 47.

3. Gerard Van Groningen, *Messianic Revelation in the Old Testament, Volume I* (Eugene, OR: Wipf and Stock, 1997), 100–103.

4. Bonhoeffer, *The Cost of Discipleship*, 47.

5. E. Murray and J. B. Murray, *And Say What He Is: The Life of a Special Child* (Cambridge, MA: MIT Press, 1975), 62–63, quoted in Helen Featherstone, *A Difference in the Family: Living with a Disabled Child* (New York: Penguin Books, 1981), 213.

6. Ibid., 213–14, Emphasis added.

Chapter 10: On Hospitality: No Room at the Inn

1. The term "hospital for sinners" comes from a quote by English Puritan Richard Sibbes: "The church of Christ is a common hospital, wherein all are in some measure sick of some spiritual disease or other; that we should all have ground of exercising mutually the spirit of wisdom and meekness." Richard Sibbes, *The Bruised Reed* (Carlisle, PA: Banner of Truth, 1998).

2. Leonard J. Vander Zee, "Making Room: The Practice of Hospitality," October 6 , 2002, http://sbcrc.org/sermons/2002.10.06.html, (November 21 , 2005).

3. Wendy Williams, email to Stephanie O. Hubach (September 16 , 2005).

Chapter 11: On Belonging: Same Body, Different Parts

1. Jean Vanier, *From Brokenness to Community* (New York: Paulist Press, 1992), 43–44.

2. Thomas E. Nicholas, "Reformed Presbyterian Church Story for Friday PM Presentation," *Sharing Christ, Showing Mercy Conference* (Atlanta: Presbyterian Church in America, March 2001), 2.

Chapter 12: On Wisdom: Questions Every Church Needs to Answer

1. Timothy J. Keller, "Session 2: The Practice of Mercy," *Sharing Christ, Showing Mercy Conference* video.(Atlanta: PCA, March 2001), Special thanks to Tim Keller for allowing me to reference his insights for this chapter.

2. Ibid.

3. Ibid.

4. Ibid.

5. Patricia K. Coiner and K. Roger Coiner, "Reformed Presbyterian Church Story for Friday PM Presentation," *Sharing Christ, Showing Mercy Conference* (Atlanta: PCA, March 2001), 2.

6. Timothy J. Keller, "Session 2: The Practice of Mercy," video.

7. Ibid.

8. Ibid.

9. Ibid.

10. Ibid.

11. Ibid.

12. Ibid.

13. Ibid.

14. Ibid.

Chapter 13: On Change: Revolution or Reformation?

1. George Grant, Grantblog, "Revolution v. Reformation," 14 March 2004, http://kingsmeadow.com (November 21, 2005).

2. Timothy J. Keller, *Ministries of Mercy: The Call of the Jericho Road* (Phillipsburg, NJ: P&R, 1997), 47.

3. Washington Gladden, "O Master Let Me Walk With Thee," 1879, http://cyberhymnal.org, (November 21, 2005).

4. Bryan Jeffrey Leech, "We Are God's People," *Trinity Hymnal*, (Atlanta: Great Commission Publications, 1990), No. 355.

Glossary

Over the course of time, disability-related terminology tends to change. The author has made every attempt to use accurate and current terminology in writing this book. Definitions of terms are listed below and also occur on the foot of the page as explanatory notes when they are first employed. If the usage of a word is unclear in the text, please refer to these definitions. Also note that the meanings of terms vary from country to country. All definitions supplied are consistent with current American disability-related terminology. This glossary is not intended to be a comprehensive glossary of disability-related terminology. It is a glossary of terms used in the context of this book.

Asperger syndrome: "Asperger syndrome (AS) is a developmental disorder that is characterized by limited interests or an unusual preoccupation with a particular subject to the exclusion of other activities. AS is an autism spectrum disorder (ASD), one of a distinct group of neurological conditions characterized by a greater or lesser degree of impairment in language and communication skills, as well as repetitive or restrictive patterns of thought and behavior." (Source: National Institute of Neurological Disorders and Stroke)

Autism: "Autism is a complex developmental disability that typically appears during the first three years of life and is the result of a neurological disorder that affects the normal functioning of the brain, impacting development in the areas of social interaction and communication skills. Both children and adults with autism typically show difficulties in verbal and non-verbal communication, social interactions, and leisure or play activities." (Source: Autism Society of America)

Cerebral palsy: "Cerebral palsy is a term used to describe a group of chronic conditions affecting body movement and muscle coordination. It is caused by damage to one or more specific areas of the brain, usually occurring during fetal development; before, during, or shortly after birth; or during infancy." (Source: United Cerebral Palsy)

Cognitive disabilities: " 'Cognitive disabilities' is often used by physicians, neurologists, psychologists and other professionals to include adults sustaining head injuries with brain trauma after age 18, adults with infectious diseases or affected by toxic substances leading to organic brain syndromes and cognitive deficits after age 18, and with older adults with Alzheimer diseases or other forms of dementias as well as other populations that do not meet the strict definition of mental retardation." Thus, *cognitive disabilities* is an "umbrella term" which includes intellectual disabilities (formerly referred to as mental retardation) but is broader than intellectual disabilities alone. (Source: U.S. Administration on Developmental Disabilities)

Developmental disabilities: "Developmental disabilities (DD) are severe, life-long disabilities attributable to mental and/or physical impairments, manifested before age 22. Developmental disabilities result in substantial limitations in three or more areas of major life activities." (Source: U.S. Administration on Developmental Disabilities)

Down syndrome: "Down syndrome is a genetic condition that causes delays in physical and intellectual development. It occurs in approximately one in every 800 live births. Individuals with Down syndrome have 47 chromosomes instead of the usual 46. It is the most frequently occurring chromosomal disorder." (Source: National Down Syndrome Association)

Intellectual disabilities: *Intellectual disabilities* is the current terminology for the condition formerly referred to as mental retardation. "Mental retardation is a disability characterized by significant limitations both in intellectual functioning and in adaptive behavior as expressed in conceptual, social, and practical adaptive skills. This disability originates before the age of 18. In regard to the intellectual criterion for the diagnosis of mental retardation, mental retardation is generally thought to be present if an individual has an IQ test score of approximately 70 or below." (Source: American Association of Mental Retardation)

Learning disabilities: "Students with learning disabilities (LD) have difficulty acquiring basic skills or academic content. Learning disabilities are characterized by intra-individual differences, usually in the form of a discrepancy between a student's ability and his or her achievement in areas such as reading, writing, mathematics, or speaking. . . . Intra-individual differences are differences within a student across academic areas. For example, a student with a LD may be quite successful in math computation and listening comprehension but may read poorly. Other students with LD may read and speak well but have difficulty expressing their thoughts in writing." (Source: Council for Exceptional Children, Division for Learning Disabilities)

Mental illness: "A mental illness is a disease that causes mild to severe disturbances in thought and/or behavior, resulting in an inability to cope with life's ordinary demands and routines. There are more than 200 classified forms of mental illness. Some of the more common disorders are depression, bipolar disorder, dementia, schizophrenia and anxiety disorders." (Source: National Mental Health Association)

Mental retardation: See definition of *intellectual disabilities.*

Multiple sclerosis: "Multiple sclerosis is a chronic, unpredictable neurological disease that affects the central nervous system." (Source: National Multiple Sclerosis Society)

Neurological disabilities: *Neurological disabilities* result from damage to the central nervous system.

Physical disabilities: *Physical disabilities* is a broad category of disability encompassing disabilities that affect movement.

Sensory disabilities: *Sensory disabilities* include deafness, blindness, or a severe vision or hearing impairment.

Spina bifida: "Spina bifida is a neural tube defect that happens in the first month of pregnancy when the spinal column doesn't close completely." (Source: Spina Bifida Association)

Spinal cord injury: "Spinal Cord Injury (SCI) is damage to the spinal cord that results in a loss of function such as mobility or feeling. Frequent causes of damage are trauma (car accident, gunshot, falls, etc.) or disease (polio, spina bifida, Friedreich's Ataxia, etc.). The spinal cord does not have to be severed in order for a loss of functioning to occur." (Source: Spinal Cord Injury Resource Center)

Stephanie O. Hubach and her husband Fred lead the disability ministry at Reformed Presbyterian Church (PCA) in Ephrata, PA. They have been married since 1983 and have two sons: Fred and Tim, who has Down syndrome. Steph has served as chairperson of the Lancaster County MH/MR Advisory Board, as a board member of The Arc of Lancaster County, as board president of the Infant Evaluation Program in Centre County, as a member of the Lancaster County Respite Coalition, and currently serves as chair of the Lancaster Christian Council on Disability.

She is a Phi Beta Kappa graduate of McDaniel College (formerly Western Maryland College), has an M.A. in economics from Virginia Polytechnic Institute and State University, and is a distance education seminary student at Covenant Theological Seminary. In her free time Stephanie likes to laugh, read, swim, and go on trips to Maine or the Jersey Shore with her family.

Stephanie frequently speaks at conferences, special events, and churches. If you would like to schedule a speaking engagement, please feel free to contact her at:

Reformed Presbyterian Church of Ephrata (RPC)
21 East Locust Street
Ephrata, Pennsylvania 17522
(717) 733-0462

For more information about the ministry of RPC, please visit
www.ephratarpc.com